BOUND TIGHTLY WITH BANANA LEAVES

Dedicated to the Burmese peoples'
struggle for democracy.

Illustrations by
Bill Stott

Photographs by
John Davies
Michael Freeman
Nicholas Greenwood
Anna McMahon
Jasper Young

Cover photograph by
John Davies

British Library Cataloguing-in-Publication Data. A catalogue record for this book is available from the British Library.

ISBN 0 9518491 0 7

© Nicholas Greenwood 1992

First published in 1992 by 'Right Now Books', 36c Sisters Avenue, London SW11 5SQ.

Distributed in the UK by Lavis Marketing, 73 Lime Walk, Headington, Oxford OX3 7AD. Tel: 0865 67575 Fax: 0865 742024

Printed by Tien Wah Press, Singapore.

BOUND TIGHTLY WITH BANANA LEAVES

A SOUTH EAST ASIAN JOURNAL

NICHOLAS GREENWOOD

RIGHT NOW BOOKS, LONDON

About the Author

Born of a French mother and a German father, Nicholas Greenwood read Modern Languages at university, but chose to leave in January 1982 to pursue a career as a horse racing journalist. He eventually became Racing Correspondent of *Pacemaker Update International*, and a freelance presenter with *Racecall*, the telephone racing service. Disillusioned with racing, he set off to Thailand in December 1989, a visit which prompted subsequent trips to the Kingdom, and thenceforth to Hong Kong, South Korea, Vietnam, Burma, Laos, Malaysia, Indonesia and Singapore. Since first setting foot onto the tarmac at Don Muang Airport, Bangkok, he has flown about sixty times either to, away or travelling within Asia.

Whilst in Thailand, he contributed to three books on Northern Thailand and the hilltribes.

Acknowledgements

I would like to thank both John Davies for unwittingly inspiring me to write this book and his ex-wife Vacharin Sirichai (Rin) for being a constant source of amazement. I also owe a special debt of gratitude to Thanomsil Khiansua (Iew) who accompanied me on the majority of my travels and tried his best – on occasions – to interpret.

I must also thank my sisters Miriam and Caroline who have staunchly put up with my travel whims, Judith Oliver, Janine Boxall and Peter Boyes for their sensible, down-to-earth advice and to David Jefferis for making the whole thing possible. Finally, to all those I met on the way (and to the Burmese I've had the pleasure of getting to know in England) and who showed typical South-East Asian hospitality, a very big 'chezu tinbada', 'kop koon kup', 'cam on nhieu', 'kop jai' and 'terima kasih'.

CONTENTS

DRAMATIS PERSONAE

The following, in order of appearance, played roles of varying degrees during my travels:

Judith Author's travel companion for a brief while.

Iew (Thanomsil Khiansua) Author's travel guide and interpreter. His name is pronounced "you".

Noi Friend of Rin, employed in Suriwong Books, Chiang Mai.

Rin (Vacharin Sirichai) Former wife of John Davies, joint owner and manageress of Rin's Guest House.

John Davies Writer, tour organiser and joint owner of Rin's Guest House.

Jos Dutch backpacker, brief inmate at Rin's Guest House.

Anthony English proprietor of a bar in Chiang Mai.

Korma Sri Lankan traveller who spent many months in Chiang Mai.

Jon Boyes English writer residing in Kiewgan, a Hmong village in Northern Thailand. He runs a small guest house with wife Sue.

Ny One of Rin's many cousins.

Moo One-time cook, waitress and cleaner at Rin's Guest House.

Peter Boyes Brother of Jon Boyes. Long-time resident in Northern Thailand.

Soda Sister of Moo and proprietress of Chiang Mai restaurant "Moo's Blues".

Nissa Divorcée and long-time resident at Rin's Guest House.

Thomas German who for a while ran a restaurant in Chiang Mai.

Louise Friend of the author, who spent a holiday in Chiang Mai.

Cheddar Friend of Rin who managed a bar in Chiang Mai.

Geneviève Goux French tour organiser based in Bangkok, specialist in Burmese affairs.

Nguyen Ngoc Sang Tour guide from Saigontourist, Ho Chi Minh City, Vietnam.

Nancy Friend of Rin who took over the running of the guest house from John Davies, funded by her Japanese husband Wattanabe.

Michel French tour operator.

Madame and Monsieur Ageing French couple who accompanied the author on his trip to Burma.

Christian and Michelle Parisian couple who joined the author on his journey to Luang Prabang, Laos.

Gonglian and Thanichai Iew's two brothers, who live in the village of Bannapho in Nakhon Phanom province, North East Thailand.

Gairo Dtah Iew's half-sister, who lives in Ban Nong Weng Yai, a remote village in Mukdahan province, North East Thailand.

Bank Friend of Iew's in Patong, Phuket.

INTRODUCTION

Thailand? Taiwan? Taipei? Taiping? Before December 1989 they were all Greek to me. But a chance journey changed all that. Like so many before me, I had fallen under the spell of the beguiling East. From the spring of 1990 to that of the following year, I spent 35 weeks travelling both within and outside the Kingdom of Thailand and found life not entirely as I had anticipated. The 'Land of Smiles' had become a land of contradictions: alluring, fascinating, infuriating and frightening.

From Thailand I ventured briefly to Hong Kong, and later to South Korea, but neither had the indefinable draw of Siam. Then to Vietnam, desperately poor but warm and welcoming. And to the great jewel of South-East Asia, Burma, where brutality, oppression, torture and murder cannot extinguish the flame of kindness. Nor diminish the awesome splendour of Pagan and Mandalay.

Poor but resilient, the people of neighbouring Laos carry on their struggle, all but cut off from the outside world. Yet in Luang Prabang, the country boasts one of the most stunning towns in all Asia. Thence over the Mekhong to 'Isaan', Thailand's forgotten region, home of giant catfish, 'sticky' rice and true Thai hospitality.

A brief stop in Penang, a contrast in bustling affluence, and on to Sumatra, a vast island of magnificent scenery and charming people. Finally, to Singapore: Asia, yes, but so far removed from the timelessness of Burma and Laos.

This, then, is an account of what I found.

PROLOGUE

"Mutter Goddams Puff in Mandelay.
Jetzt ruht ueber Dir die grucne See.
Goddam, was war das fuer ein
   Etablissement!
Jetzt stehen keine fuenf mehr die
   Bretterwand entlang.
Jetzt gibts keine Uhr und kein Hohe!
Und kein Mensch mehr ist in Mandelay.
Damals gabs noch Menschen auf der
  . Welt
Und die waren damals wert ihr Geld.
Jetzt ist eben nichts mehr auf der Welt
   in Ordnung
Und ein Puff, wie dieses kennt man heut
   nicht mehr.
Keinen Browning mehr und auch kein
   Tuerchen,
Wo kein Mensch ist, da ist auch kein
   Verkehr.
Rascher, Johnny, he
Rascher, Johnny, he
Stimmt ihn an, den Song von Mandelay
Liebe, die ist doch an Zeit nicht gebun-
   den,
Johnny, mach raschen, denn hier gehts
   um Sekunden.
Ewig nicht stehet der Mond ueber Dir,
   Mandelay
Ewig nicht stehet der Mond ueber Dir."

"Mother Goddam's joint in Mandalay.
Now the green sea washes over it.
Hell, what a place that was!
Now nobody is lined up by the partition.
Now there are no clocks and no shouts
And there's nobody left in Mandalay.
Once there were real people in the
   world
And once they were worth their cash.
Now, precisely nothing in the world is
   OK
And a joint like that is unknown.
No gun, no little door,
Where there's nobody, there's no
   traffic.
Hurry, Johnny,
Hurry, Johnny,
Let's sing The Song of Mandalay.
Love knows no boundaries of time,
Johnny, hurry up, for every second
   counts here.
Mandalay, the moon doesn't always
   stand over you.
Mandalay, the moon doesn't always
   stand over you."

(Bertolt Brecht, Happy End).

You will have all heard of Burma, but not so many will know of Myanmar, its new name. And some of you will be aware of the military's heinous crimes against the peoples of Burma.

Anyone who has been fortunate enough to visit this beautiful land couldn't fail to be enchanted by the magnificence of the temples and, above all, by the indescribable kindness of the Burmese. And at the same time moved by their plight. Two organizations have been established in the UK to assist the Burmese: the non-political Prospect Burma, a trust set up to educate and train young Burmese who have been compelled to flee their country, and the Burma Action Group UK (BAG UK), which aims to restore democracy in Burma. It is a long, hard struggle but if you are at all interested in their cause, do contact either (or both) groups. The addresses are:

     Prospect Burma, 138 Victoria Rise, London SW4 0NW
     BAG UK, 1a Bonny Street, London NW1 9PE

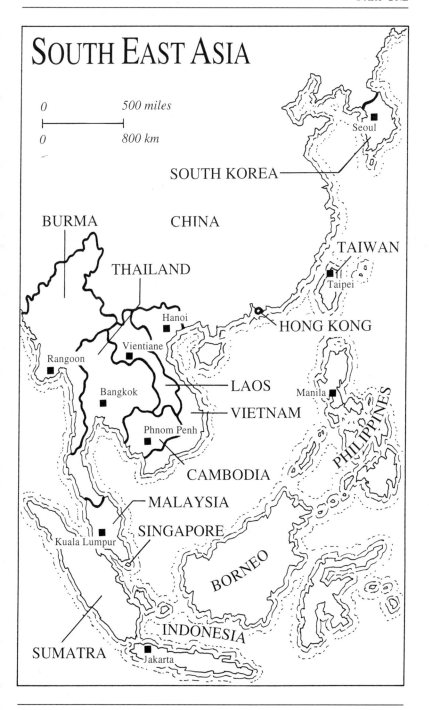

SOUTH EAST ASIA

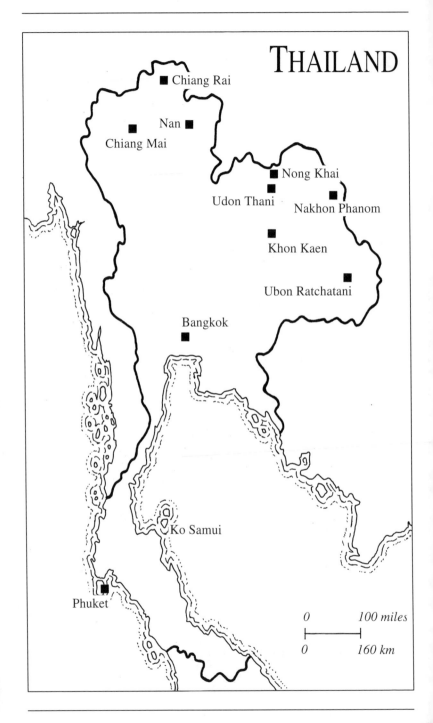

THAILAND

Chiang Rai

Nan

Chiang Mai

Nong Khai

Udon Thani

Nakhon Phanom

Khon Kaen

Ubon Ratchatani

Bangkok

Ko Samui

Phuket

| 0 | 100 miles |
| 0 | 160 km |

PART ONE

CHIANG MAI AND MORE . . .

"Ich war jung, Gott, erst sechzehn
  Jahre
Du kamest von Burma herauf
Du sagtest, ich solle mit dir gehen
Du kaemest fuer alles auf . . .
. . . Du sagtest viel, Johnny
Kein Wort war wahr, Johnny
Du has mich betrogen, Johnny'
Zur ersten Stund.
Ich hasse dich so, Johnny
Wie du da stehst und grinst, Johnny
Nimm doch die Pfeife aus dem Maul,
  du Hund!"

"I was young, God, only sixteen
You came up from Burma
You told me I should go with you
You would take care of everything . . .
. . . You said so much, Johnny
Not a word was true, Johnny
You deceived me, Johnny
From the very first moment
I hate you so, Johnny
As you stand there grinning, Johnny
Take that pipe out of your gob, you
  dog!"
(Bertolt Brecht, Happy End)

Tuesday, 6th March:
Bangkok, Thailand: Miami Hotel, the room: three hundred and twenty-five baht a cockroach. And food poisoning courtesy of Thai Airways International. Their free orchid smiles at me knowingly from the bedside table. Summon a doctor: his English is fluent enough to request a thousand baht. He sticks something in my arm which he says is glucose but he's Thai and I'm convinced he's trying to do away with me. What a welcome.

Wednesday, 7th March:
Judith discovers the 'delights' of Bangkok (alone) on a whirlwind three hour tour. In that time maybe she'll get to the end of the 'soi'. Tells me she's seen a 'real' pearl factory — her taxi driver's words. I hope she wasn't tempted to part with her cash — whatever the price. A Thai taxi driver's phrase–book consists of roughly four expressions:
  "Hello, where you come from?"
  "How long you stay?"
  "You want massage?"
  "You want lady or boy?"
Oh yes, and useful words like *"discount"*, *"special"*, and *"price"* and not forgetting the ubiquitous *"I know velly good hotel for you"*. Funny, my Charles Berlitz cassette only teaches me phrases like *"Mr Daeng isn't at home"*.

Thursday, 8th March:
Return to Phuket and Seaview Hotel. Patong Beach is abuzz — with pineapple sellers, purveyors of massage, boys offering umbrellas, sunglasses, wallets, T–shirts, sandwiches (which, by now, must be rancid): there is a never ending stream. Most welcome of all are the newspaper boys: *"Italiano, Italiano,"* they holler at me. *"Angrit,"* I reply and a look of disappointment comes over their faces. They've run out of the *Bangkok Post*, but have numerous copies of a two-week-old Italian daily. And finally the women, in their conical Vietnamese–style hats, proffering drinks. Poor girls spend all day walking up and down the beach in the scorching heat, each repeating *"Would you like some dlink?"* to every 'farang'.

Saturday, 10th March:
Laze on the beach all day and get burnt. In the evening — against my better judgement — we have been persuaded to watch the famous Thai boxing ('Muay Thai') at a stadium in Phuket Town. Our minibus manages to knock down two motor cyclists at the same time. We all get out and wait while our driver — who claims to be innocent and doesn't flee the scene (there's a turn–up) — is removed. We are temporarily stranded by the side of the road, awaiting a replacement driver. The boxing is an anti–climax: the benches are bad for piles, the locals scream and jump about through every bout, and the wailing music is reminiscent of an Indian restaurant I used to frequent in London. The boxer I tipped isn't a patch on our minibus driver and fails to knock over anything.

Experienced Thai driving at its finest.

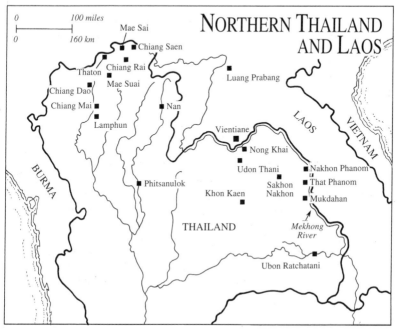

Sunday, 11th March:
The stadium's benches have left me numb in places. I think the whole performance lasted about five hours.

Take a boat to a nearby beach and for a while we sit quite alone. But the next arrival brings in two awful Cockney couples, who are sure to sit next to me. I think they are secondhand car salesmen from Romford.

Monday, 12th March:
"Italiano, Italiano?" "No, Angrit" "Rundon Standard?" I can't quite believe it and fleetingly imagine myself to be on the forecourt of Waterloo Station and not Patong Beach. But there it is — Friday's *Standard.* But at eighty baht — a mark–up of around eight hundred and fifty per cent — I turn it down. And in any case, I want the 'West End Final' and not the 'City' edition.

Thursday, March 15th:
The Phuket days are over — at least for the time being. Reluctantly we must return to Bangkok: Judith is heading for Australia. And as for me — well, who knows?
 The taxi–driver to the airport is a maniac. *"Not casey,"* says my guide Iew. *"Thai."*

Saturday, March 17th:
Decide to seek my fortune in Chiang Mai — as a teacher. Iew and I check in at the seedy Hotel Montha, a real snip at two hundred and eighty baht. The hotel is recommended for its proximity to the Night Bazaar and . . . well, little else. The shower water appears to come straight from Alaska, cold enough to freeze the balls off any nosey cockroach that dares poke up through the plumbing.

Monday, March 19th:
Do the rounds of the language schools in Chiang Mai — armed with my CV, which neatly omits to mention that I dropped out of university. After a couple of failures, I end up at ECC (English Conversation Club) in the north west of the city. I don't know why but they seem impressed, or maybe plain-desperate. *"So you speak Falench and Yermun?"* the manageress asks. *"Yes, fluently,"* I reply, crossing my fingers under the table. They have two girls who want to improve their French — I try to convince myself that my French *must* surely be better than theirs, and rush out and borrow a secondhand English–French dictionary. I am also given an English class with an apparently unspecified number of pupils who have learned the language for two years. Now at least that should be OK. . .

Tuesday, 20th March:
Late lunch and diarrhoea.

Wednesday, 21st March:
Today it all went horribly wrong. I am supposed to embark on my teaching career but am doubled up with stomach–ache — and the 'squits'. Reel into school at four thirty for my first class at six o'clock, only to be greeted by a girl inquiring *"Where you go?"* (should I tell her that she's in the wrong tense?).

"What you mean 'where I go?' I come here for lesson." I explain in my best broken English.

"But lesson at fy, not sick. You late. Girl go."
It's no use telling her that I was instructed to turn up at six o'clock *not* five o'clock. At least she can't shout at me or sack me — no, that's taboo over here. Neither of us must lose face. So she proffers the usual and irritating 'mai ben lai' ('never mind') and asks me to come back at five o'clock tomorrow. I can see it's going to be a struggle simply coming to terms with the staff, let alone the pupils.

Thursday, 22nd March:
First day as 'Mr Nick, khun kroo' — the teacher. I am French tutor to two charming twenty–year–old girls, whose command of the language is distinctly modest. I make sure I remain one step ahead at all times by keeping the dictionary on my lap and frantically — but surreptitiously — looking up words for the coming topics. They don't seem to notice.

Sunday, 25th March:
Ah the weekend, but have to be up early for my first English class. There are four students — at last count they told me five — who are all girls from Phitsanulok, wherever that may be.

"So you've studied English for two years?" I inquire hopefully. Silence and blank looks. Foolish of me, of course, to use the past tense. *"You learn English two year?"*

One girl casts off her timidity. *"No, two week."*

Horror and panic. *"Mai ben lai,"* I reply. They giggle nervously. I shuffle my notes together, put them away and smile for what seems like an eternity. They can barely understand a word, and I've got to go on like this for two hours. I suppose I can talk gibberish so long as I grin at them knowingly.

I get by, but will surely run out of conversation. Am too knackered to agree a price with the 'tuk–tuk' driver — and so get ripped off. What a day: I'd like to say 'mai ben lai', but swear violently instead.

Monday, 26th March:
Today's English class attracts six girls and two boys. The majority can't understand a word. I just don't know how long I can keep this up.

Tuesday, 27th March:
Decide to move from Hotel Montha to a guest house — 'geh how' as the Thais say — in a 'soi' just off the Night Bazaar. It's recommended by a charming Thai lady — called Noi — who works in the shop where I buy my *Bangkok Post* each day.

"How much you pay in Montha Hotel?" she asks.

"Two hundred and eighty baht a day," I reply.

"Oh too much, Lin geh how velly cheap. Lin velly good fliend for me."

The establishment actually goes under the name of Rin's Guest House and is run by Rin, a pretty Thai lady in her thirties. Her family comes from the nearby town of Lamphun and she tells me she is of Burmese and Chinese origin. Her husband — a writer called John Davies — is also an ex–teacher, marine biologist, actor, lecturer and 'Scrabble' fanatic. He has recently finished a book on the hilltribes of Northern Thailand — a subject which means little to me but is apparently the reason why so many tourists flock to Chiang Mai — and bears a remarkable likeness to Michael Palin.

Rin is only charging one hundred and eighty baht a night — discounted to three thousand a month — for a double room with air conditioning, and at this time of the year, that's an absolute essential. On the top floor are a Chinese–looking lad and two Thai girls who work in the Night Bazaar. There's also a Dutchman by the name of Jos (pronounced Yos) who talks too much.

Thursday, 29th March:
I was right about the Dutchman. Worse than his incessant chat — he smells and never changes his T–shirt. Either that or he's got an entire wardrobe of black T–shirts. Today he appears from his room stoned on marijuana and doesn't shut up, analysing every word I utter. Rin doesn't like him: *"Fucking man from Holland. Talk too much bullshit."* She has a way with the English language, acquired, cynics might say, in a bar of ill repute.

Jos persuades John to take him up into the hilltribes to help with his latest book — a hilltribe phrase–book. Apparently all the tribes have their own particular language. For John's sake I hope Jos changes his T–shirt.

Tuesday, 3rd April:
John and the mad Dutchman return from the hills (sounds like a scene from *The Sound of Music*). I don't think it was a great success. Attempting to write a phrase–book which can be used by European, American and antipodean travellers alike is a daunting task.

It's blisteringly hot and we are all looking forward to 'Songkran' in ten days time, the Thai New Year when Chiang Mai will be packed and every-one chucks water at you.

Thursday, 5th April:
The Dutchman should leave today — he's found a cheaper 'geh how'. John and I organise the weekend trip — my first visit to the hilltribes. School is just so frustrating — neither of my four o'clock class decides to turn up. The girl (who blushes each time I look at her — I fear she's in love with me) has gone shopping instead, and no one knows what's happened to the boy, who goes under the bizarre name of 'Rag'.

Friday, 6th April:
Relations between John and Rin are rather strained.

Saturday, 7th April:
I'm somewhere in the hills of Northern Thailand. I say 'somewhere' because we are lost in the environs of Doi Inthanon, Thailand's highest mountain. We were supposed to spend the night in a Karen village but we couldn't find it. Still I didn't really fancy spending the night on the floor of a malarial hut. On the way back some kids on the side of the road hurl water at the jeep and soak us. So this is 'Songkran' — one week early.

I am beginning to suspect that the hitherto delightful Rin isn't all she seems.

Sunday, 8th April:
John and Rin are at it hammer and tongs — arguing that is. Go to her parents' house at Lamphun and she refuses to return to Chiang Mai with us. We stop off at a bar run by a Cockney chap called Anthony who treats his Thai wife like dirt. Anthony tells John that he's much too soft with Rin and he mustn't let her get her way. *"Tread on her,"* he says, *"she's Thai."* I ask him about concepts such as *"loyalty", "trust"* and *"fidelity"*. *"All bollocks,"* comes the truculent reply.

So without dithering too much, John takes Anthony's advice and decides to give Rin the boot. Now she's packing up all her gear. John and I, meanwhile, return to Anthony's bar where he wastes no time picking up a girl he's fancied for ages. Assuming that Rin has gone home to Lamphun, he drives to the guest house. To his horror, Rin — in a performance not far removed from that of Lady Macbeth — is sitting outside the 'geh how' with a plaintive look on her tear–stained face. Misery turns swiftly to rage as she espies the girl in the front seat of the jeep. *"Fucking butterfly . . . farang no fucking good"* she screams and hurls her wedding ring into the gutter — never to be seen again. John speeds up past the guest house, swearing violently. The girl is understandably bemused as we drop her back at Anthony's bar. *"Farang casey,"* she mutters. Maybe that's what the expression 'short time' means.

Meanwhile, the demented Rin has rushed upstairs in a flood of tears. *"Now I kill mysel,"* she wimpers and locks herself in one of the bedrooms.

All that remains is for her to reappear, clad in a nightgown, sleepwalking and uttering *"Is this a meat cleaver I see before me?"*.

Needless to say, she doesn't 'do the deed'.

Tuesday, 10th April:
John and Rin appear to have patched things up. Everyone in the 'geh how' is *"velly happy"*, especially Iew, who calmly pronounces *"I die in two year. I see doctor in Patong and he say I die in two year."* I inquire why — and he can't offer me an explanation. So tomorrow we'll pay a visit to the Lanna Hospital. Maybe I'll soon awake from this weird dream that is Thailand.

Wednesday, 11th April:
"No die," announces Iew unconcernedly as he saunters into the guest house. Oh, who can comprehend the Thai mentality?

Friday, 13th April:
Friday the 13th and the start of 'Songkran'. The streets are thronging with Thais and 'farangs', who are considered fair game for a drenching. It's impossible to venture beyond the end of the 'soi' without getting soaked. Those who have been in Chiang Mai for past New Years wrap their cameras and wallets in plastic bags and stuff them in their pockets. But that offers scant protection against the buckets, water pistols, vats and hoses. *"Songkran, Songkran,"* they shout as they tip freezing water — with ice–cubes for good measure — down your neck. At least the temperature in Chiang Mai is in the nineties.

The Songkran Water Festival.

Saturday, 14th April:
Tonight John, Rin, Iew, Korma — a Sri Lankan lad who speaks English at a rate of knots, never shuts up and is desperately tight with his baht ('kee niaow', as the Thais say) — and I have been invited to a traditional Chiang Mai house–warming party. We must dress in local costume, which consists of a collar–less blue linen shirt and a type of cummerbund — I don't think they care about the trousers.

Someone had erroneously told us that the water–drenching stops at six o'clock, for we get soaked again. At this time of the evening it's no longer amusing, and it's also dangerous to traffic as you instinctively shut your eyes to avoid the flying gallons. We pray we won't have to linger too long at the traffic lights, but to no avail as they turn to red in front of us. There, waiting to pounce, is a group of Thais armed with a cauldron. *"Mai ao, mai ao,"* we plead, beg, implore. Their smiles turn to fury: they say something to us in Thai, shake their fists and speed off. Rin explains: *"Farang cannot say no to water when Songkran. They angry. I think maybe they want to kill you. This time you lucky."* Ah, 'Songkran', 'Songkran' . . .

Wednesday, 18th April:
Teaching is getting me down. I'm finding it hard to think up new topics each day. The school has no material to work with, and if I want to make photo-copies of the few books they do have, I must pay for them myself. So I decide to give it up: I get Rin to phone up on my behalf to tell them I'm sick. I don't think they believe her. Each day they telephone the guest house enquiring about me. Eventually Rin has enough: *"This time I fucking tell them."* And she did.

I asked her what she told the school.
   "I say your wife not like you go to school. I say your wife, she jealous of girl in school. They Thai, they understand."

With school scrapped, I am now free to help John with his latest book — the hilltribe phrasebook. There are six major tribes — Akha, Hmong (or Meo), Karen, Lahu, Lisu, Yao (or Mien) — all with their different cultures, customs and, perhaps most interestingly, languages. Communication, there-fore, is almost impossible, particularly as many do not speak Thai. And very few tourists who have travelled specifically to Northern Thailand to explore the tribes speak Thai in any case.

So we set out by jeep for Chiang Rai, north of Chiang Mai and an excel-lent base for research. Chiang Rai itself gets mixed reports: the hippies and backpackers love to hang out there, but I found it an ugly, uninspiring town. It lacks the charm of Chiang Mai and, save its position, has very little going for it.

We travel on to the Burmese border at Mae Sai. This is an extraordinary town, a real dusty old outpost, with an abundance of sellers and buyers. Thais and Burmese can cross the border, which in effect is a bridge over the stream that separates the two lands, and leads to Tachilek. Thais pass through frequently to avail themselves of cheap Burmese goods, while the Burmese come over possibly to experience 'democracy' for a day. Tourists are forbidden to cross the border, though it must be quite tempting to wade through the water to the other side. I've heard the tale of a Japanese — who bore a resemblance to a Thai — who sauntered nonchalantly past the border patrols into Burma without so much as a by your leave. It wasn't so easy on his return to Thailand, however, as the guard asked him in Thai for his ID. Unable to understand a word, he was promptly fined two thousand baht. Still at least he'd experienced autocracy.

Mae Sai is a hawker's paradise, particularly as Burma conjures up this magical and mysterious image. There is an especially large supply of gems; indeed there are stalls everywhere. *"Loobies from Burma"* the girls are offering at remarkable prices. More disturbing than these copies, perhaps, are the pretty young Thai girls — no more than eight or nine years old — who claim to be from the hilltribes. They are clad in fake costumes and demand ten baht to be photographed. John asks one girl which tribe she's from: she shrugs her shoulders. Their outfits are garish but in no way authentic: I wonder who's profiting from this charade?

Thursday, 19th April:
We drive on to the so–called 'Golden Triangle', where the borders of Thailand, Burma and Laos converge. The name 'Golden Triangle' evokes images of bellicose drug barons and basket–loads of poppies, but there's no evidence of that here. There's a large cement sign marking the spot, which is actually on the Mekhong River eleven kilometres north of the town of Chiang Saen. Once again there are souvenir stalls to satisfy the needs of every tourist. The 'Golden Triangle' area, a poppy–growing mountainous region, whilst technically indefinable, is considered to radiate out from the village of Sop Ruak, stretching south almost to Chiang Mai and north towards Yunnan province in China, and encompassing North West Laos and the Shan States of Burma.

Chiang Saen, overlooking the Mekhong, is a marvellously scenic spot and we lunch there. After, we head on towards a Hmong village (Kiewgan), where a writer friend of John's — called Jon Boyes — lives with his Thai wife Sue. Jon — an expert on the Hmong hilltribe — hails originally from Grayshott and rents out his spare room at thirty baht a night to any traveller who can make it up to his village and who fancies spending the night on the floor. This zero star but nonetheless hospitable accommodation goes under the name of 'The Hmong Guest House'. Jon has written books on the Hmong tribe, and we sit and chat. I find it quite incongruous to be seated on the verandah of a hut somewhere in Northern Thailand, with oil lamps offering the sole means of light and surrounded by two guys from the south of England.

Friday, 20th April:
I don't think any of us slept much last night. We return to Chiang Rai over the bumpiest path I've ever been bounced up and down upon. I think it's mainly motorbikes that venture up to the village. The Hmong have been charming and seem to have accepted the 'farang' into their midst. He has plans to build a larger guest house, which should benefit the villagers financially — as long as the trekking companies can be kept away.

Spend the night at the grotty but quaintly named 'Poppy Inn', overpriced at two hundred and eighty baht for a room with fan.

Saturday, 21st April:
Return to Chiang Mai.

Monday, 23rd April:
Today finally make it to Doi Suthep, which has wonderful views of the city, but, like so many tourist sights in the Kingdom, is marred by hawkers and souvenir stalls. And nearby Doi Pui, where there is a so–called hilltribe village (allegedly Hmong) sums up all that's wrong with the tourist trade. It's just pure exploitation, simply a shop–window of hilltribe wares, and yet tourists are taken there in droves to witness hilltribe 'life' and to be shown poppy fields which don't appear to have any poppies. *"Oh no,"* my guide informs me, *"poppy season finish."*

Wednesday, 25th April:
Depart for the North–East, or 'Isaan' as the Thais call it. 'Isaan' is the huge chunk of Thailand which tourists shun, where they speak Lao and eat 'sticky' rice ('kao niaow'), where the real poverty of the Kingdom is, but where the people are the most genuine, untainted by tourism. 'Isaan' is where, in all probability, your 'tuk–tuk' driver in Bangkok is from, and so many of the bar–girls. The majestic Mekhong flows through the region, marking the border with the forgotten land of Laos on its muddy way from the South China Sea via Vietnam and Cambodia.

Our route to the North–East takes us on an old Thai Airways Shorts 330 propeller plane via Khon Kaen — the largest city in 'Isaan' — to Sakhon Nakhon. At Khon Kaen, all bar Iew and I disembark, leaving the air hostess with a dilemma. She knows she ought to begin her announcement with "ladies and gentlemen", but with no ladies aboard isn't sure what to say. *"Gentlemen . . ."* she proudly asserts . . . and then has to sit down, overcome with giggles. After thirty-five minutes, we touch down at Sakhon Nakhon Airport, which is in truth little more than a military airstrip. Our eventual destination is the border town of Nakhon Phanom, a former US base, and some ninety kilometres north east of Sakhon Nakhon.

Sakhon Nakhon Airport is all but deserted: I was hoping for a bus, but there's nothing. They seem to be shutting up shop for the day. *"Bus to Nakhon Phanom?"* I inquire optimistically, expecting the response *"sorry, bus go already."* Not so. *"Sorry, no have bus. You take Thai Airways taxi — only seven hundred baht."* I should have guessed it; other than spending the night in Sakhon Nakhon, I have no choice.

On the road to Nakhon Phanom.

The driver is a maniac. We stop to refuel at a petrol station and I politely suggest I move from the front seat to the back compartment. He seems bemused, but seeing as he knows no English and my 'Isaan' is dodgy, there's no discussion. *"Farang passart,"* (mad) he mutters. I shut my eyes as he deftly avoids the water buffalo that wander nonchalantly onto the road. I wonder what Nakhon Phanom will be like — and whether I'll be alive to see it.

Thursday, 27th April:
Save for its marvellously craggy views of Laos and the Mekhong, Nakhon Phanom offers little. Few tourists venture here these days but it has a certain charm that is simply 'Isaan' — the food, the dialect and the people. The town has many Vietnamese refugees, as well as Laotians, who cross the river each day. We, alas, cannot. But we climb down to the river and

walk over the dried up banks of the Mekhong as far as possible. It's the dry season now and we feel we can almost reach the mysterious land that lies so near.

Saturday, 28th April:
Take a 'songthaew' to Iew's village, Bannapho which is about forty-five minutes outside Nakhon Phanom. It is quite a large village on either side of the road to Sakhon Nakhon. One part is home to a large Lao refugee camp; his house is on the other side of the road. *"Farang, farang,"* the kids scream as I arrive, as if I'm some latter–day Dr Livingstone. They seem to appear from nowhere. They stare and stare as I sit on the floor — and smile and giggle. Only one person — a woman in her fifties or sixties — speaks any English. She reminisces about Laos and the Vietnam War, the time when the town served as a US Air Force base. And there are more obvious signs, too: a boy, much darker than the Thais or Laotians, whose father was a black US soldier and mother from Bannapho. He is Thai in all but physical appearance, but his father has long since gone and he speaks no English.

Sunday, 29th April:
Return to Chiang Mai. The atmosphere at Rin's is much the same. But I have a proposal to put to the warring factions. I wish to purchase a share of the guest house, in order that I can have a base. Rin, naturally, thinks I'm mad. She is deeply suspicious and feels that I am usurping her authority. I wonder how all this will affect her ever increasing insanity?

Tuesday, 1st May:
John leaves on another trek to the 'Golden Triangle' — don't people want to go anywhere else? Book flight to Hong Kong for later in the month: I've decided to visit some friends there and renew my visa.

Friday, 4th May:
In John's absence, the mad Rin has calmed down. Today the lawyer is coming over to discuss my offer to buy a share of the guest house. I've suggested a sum of five thousand pounds. That should get her going again. And true to form, Rin gives the lawyer short shrift and promptly disappears when it's time to sign the papers. Eventually she does put pen to paper and then goes off in another huff. This one looks set to last some time.

Saturday, 5th May:
To pacify the 'Mad One', John buys her a baby mynah bird. It neither talks nor flies, but merits the name 'Korma' simply because one day they anticipate it being an incessant chatterbox.

Sunday, 6th May:
John and I head off in search of some hilltribe villages: we fail to find any interesting ones, but I do see my first snake.

Monday, 7th May:
Discover an outstanding Akha village, and then return to Chiang Rai where we spend the night in a fifty baht 'geh how'.

Tuesday, 8th May:
A day of traumas. Firstly, the jeep refuses to start. It's been playing up for some time and today it just won't budge. So we have to track down a mechanic in Chiang Rai; there are several guys willing to help, but they mostly smile and stare at the engine. After three hours of tinkering, one lad pronounces the jeep fit to drive. We abandon the game of 'Scrabble' we were playing on the pavement and set off in search of a Yao village. The jeep goes OK, but not us, alas, and we lose our way. Eventually we find our bearings and return via a Lisu village.

The sky is beginning to look menacing, and John puts his foot down in an attempt to beat the storm. He hasn't told me before, but lightning terrifies him and he starts to shake and panic as the heavens light up with the most amazing tropical storm I've ever witnessed. 'Songkran' is mere child's play as the skies empty: the road ahead is flooded almost at once and the way ahead is a blur. *"We must find a house. I've got to stop."* He is trembling, in dread. *"But there's nothing here,"* I reply. *"And anyway we can't see anything because of the rain."* Panic isn't far away as the lightning seems almost upon us. *"I'm fucking stopping,"* he bellows and veers violently off the road. Thank God nothing's coming the other way. We end up in someone's drive. *"I hope the natives are friendly."* We knock on the door and proffer a hopeful *"Sawatdee, kup"*.

"Fontok mak mak. Kao kang nai dee kwar," comes the reply. John and I look at each other blankly. Well 'fontok' means 'rain' but the rest . . . God knows? We enter: it's like walking into a weird funeral wake. There are three boys sitting and smoking, but not talking. We are offered an unripe mango each — fortunately John has his Swiss army knife handy. The mangoes are inedible — but we make an attempt. We sit in silence for twenty minutes until the storm abates. The back of the jeep is flooded, the engine luckily not. We say our thank–you's and continue on our way. The natives were friendly . . . if a little strange.

Wednesday, 9th May:
A mynah bird lands on my window–sill: this causes a commotion amongst the staff as the mad Rin, abandoning her customers, rushes upstairs in an attempt to lure the creature into her shopping basket. *"Friend for Korma,"* she shrieks. *"I wait for bird to go into basket. Good, na?"* Clearly the bird felt it didn't want to enter the witch's cauldron: it flew off shortly afterwards to howls of horror from Rin.

Friday, 11th May:
John and Rin aren't speaking to each other — but that's nothing unusual. It may have something to do with the fact that yesterday we concluded our deal on the guest house. I now own a share of 'Rin's Rooms for Rent' as the letters alliterate on the front of the building. Rin may be deeply suspicious and resentful, but that doesn't stop her spending my money freely. *"We go shopping. Buy everything new."* We return with an air–conditioner and a fridge. John and Rin then stage a slanging match while I'm engrossed in conversation with a charming English woman from West Hampstead — one of the few 'farangs' who haven't been scared away by the 'Mad One'. Midway through exchanging nostalgia about England, I hear a thud from outside the guest house. Has Rin finally done the deed? No, it is Ny, one of her many cousins (which reminds me of an incident in the guest house when a friend of Rin's called by, desperate for money. She refused to help him, stating quite bluntly: *"I not help him. He not my cousin."* This probably explains why everyone in Thailand is someone's cousin). Anyway back to Ny: he is slumped on the side of the 'soi', unconscious and with blood oozing out of his mouth. Iew and Moo (at two weeks, the longest serving cook in Rin's) bundle him into a 'tuk–tuk', which then stops halfway down the 'soi' and reverses, screeching, back to the guest house. *"No have money,"* Iew yells frantically. I hurl a few notes at the 'tuk–tuk' and they disappear. I fear the end is Ny.

Two hours later, Iew and Moo — which sounds rather like a Thai version of Sooty and Sweep — return, minus Ny. *"No problem, don't worry,"* Iew says in the plaintive tone that Thais seem to perfect. *"Ny not die."* The whole scene resembles something out of a third rate tragicomedy.

Saturday, 12th May:
Ny has discharged himself from hospital. Apparently he has a liver problem — and when he gets drunk, he passes out. But no word of thanks for (a) rescuing him (b) rushing him to hospital or (c) paying for the 'tuk–tuk'. I keep thinking what an extraordinary race the Thais are. Any country whose favourite TV cartoon star is a *boy* called 'Icky Sue' must be odd.

Today is FA Cup Final day — and we get live coverage. The Thais are wild about football and seem more excited than us 'farangs'. Iew, too, is 'excited' — but for different reasons. I have accidentally locked him in the shower. Being Thai, he believes it was intentional.

Sunday, 13th May:
Jon Boyes' brother Peter turns up: he has a reputation in Chiang Mai for being a layabout and a philanderer. That is tempting fate in a city where seventy-five per cent of the prostitutes are thought to be HIV positive. Peter is actually charming — well–known for breaking many a bar–girl's heart.

Rin hates him — *"he butterfly, he fuck around"* — so he must be a nice chap. The demented one is in a particularly foul mood: there'll be trouble soon.

Monday, 14th May:
Troops have been summoned, swords are being drawn: let battle commence. This woman's off her bloody trolley, a psychiatrist's nightmare. Unpredictable. It seems there is no sense behind anything she does. And yet at times she can be so calculating — an all too familiar trait amongst bar–girls (not that Rin was one — so I'm told). I have noticed in many Thais the same characteristics: several just don't seem to have grown up. They are children at heart — capricious, irresponsible and wanton. They are like a spoiled kid who one day must have a new train set, the next day a pair of shoes. And Rin encapsulates all these qualities — she has no idea how to run a business, she never keeps accounts (nor staff). And yet you can't criticise her because then she would lose face, which, like so many things in this frustrating land, is taboo. So poor John can only watch and despair as his business — part of which, alas, is mine — and his relationship go down the drain. The tally of 'farang'/Thai liaisons which have fallen apart — often with horrifying consequences — is incredibly high.

But back to the performance: she storms out like a child frustrated in her desires. John goes off too, on the pretext of acquiring a birdcage for Korma (who has outgrown his shopping basket) and I, so to speak, am left holding the baby.

The mad Rin.

Late at night: the mad axe–woman of Lamphun finally flips. I am in my room reading, but rush downstairs on hearing a commotion. An apparition even more hideous than that of the dagger–wielding Macbeth greets me: it is she, frenzied, brandishing a meat–cleaver. *"I kill him, I kill him. He fucking butterfly. I kill him."* Moo is desperately trying to pacify her, but Rin will not be distracted from her path — revenge her sole ambition. *"Nick, Nick,"* Moo yells frantically, *"you tell her. John not butterfry."* *"Me?"* It is a foolish interception — like some reptilian monster out of Dr Who, Rin turns round quickly to face me: *"You,"* she shrieks, *"I kill you. John not here, he go butterfly with girl. I kill you."* Meanwhile, Iew has appeared and, together with Moo, they attempt to reason with the weapon–wielding maniac. As for me, in the best British manner — and judging by the accident reports in the *Bangkok Post* — Thai too, decide to flee the scene. Scampering upstairs, frenetic, I shove what I can into my backpack and formulate my escape. I can still hear the shrieks from the corridor. Then, with wonderful sang–froid, John strolls into the guest house. He has just been to the hospital with Jon and Peter Boyes — and Jon's wife, Sue. Sue, foolishly, chose to sit in the front of the jeep: and any female in the front seat of John's jeep is just asking for gelding in this 'Land of Smiles'.

I stay, but decide to terminate the contract. John just doesn't know what to do. He feels sorry for Rin, but then he wasn't within range of the meat–cleaver. I feel disgust — and distrust. She has lost all respect and dignity — and, worst of all for the Thais — lost face. Later, he confides in me — yes, his marriage is over, but he will keep on Rin as manager of the guest house (if she can be bothered to get out of bed, that is) on a monthly salary of five thousand baht. John, now, reveals his true feelings: he lives in terror, in fear for his life. He is convinced she wants to do away with him. He implores me to feign fondness towards Rin to save his scalp and — not least of all — his money. *"You know,"* he tells me, *"she may well burn down the guest house."* This he says with a perfectly straight face. So, I go to my room and remove the grilles from the windows — you can never be too sure. This may be the 'Land of Smiles', but it's said that Thailand has one of the highest domestic murder rates in the world. And I don't intend to be another statistic. Nor, I sense, does John.

Tuesday, 15th May:
The night has passed without assassination or conflagration. Instead, all the staff have decided to leave, Rin included. Moo departs — along with the two thousand five hundred baht I lent to clear her debts — but in the end, alas, not Rin. All day they talk — John desperately looking for a way to save his investment, and Rin . . . well I doubt if even the most eminent Harley Street physician could make her out.

Poor Moo has had a terrible time of it. Part owner — with her appropriately named sister Soda — of the very popular restaurant in Chiang Mai called 'Moo's Blues' (another apt and foreboding title), her life has been anything but 'sanuk'. A failed marriage behind her, alas poor Moo was betrayed in wholesome Thai–style by her sister who kicked her out of the restaurant and pocketed the takings into the bargain. So the hapless Moo — ever cheerful but nonetheless more down–to–earth and realistic than most of her race — ended up at Rin's, veritably out of the frying–pan into the fire.

Jon, Peter and Sue are off to Bangkok on the overnight bus. Jon hopes to get a UK visa for Sue. We sit and chat: they think Rin is crazy and dangerous. They tell me I should flee while I'm still (physically) unscathed. We all go out to supper near the Night Bazaar — moody Rin says nothing, merely glaring at Sue in that suspicious Thai way. We drop them off at the bus station — Rin stays in the jeep and, by the time we've said our farewells, she has disappeared. John is in a frenzy again: I do my best to calm him down. *"It's all a game,"* I assure him. (Someone once told me that the Thais were the best actors — or in Rin's case tragedienne — in the world).

And lo and behold, there she is, waiting for us in the guest house which was once her great domain. Now it's all falling apart. John has decided to remove her for a week's holiday. Taking no chances, I spend the night at the nearby Diamond Hotel.

Wednesday, 16th May:
I return in the morning to find John — Rin–free — in conversation with the lawyer. Apparently Rin wants the lease of the guest house in her name. So there's a new twist: she is clearly trying to milk the poor man for all he's got. As each day passes, he is growing more and more anxious, fidgety, neurotic. He seems to be losing all track of reality. *"She's going to kill us all, I'm sure,"* he jabbers. *"We've all got to get away at once."* I can't believe what I'm hearing: it sounds like a Thai version of 'Escape from Devil's Island'. *"I know a place: Nan."* *"Nan? I thought that was something you ate with chicken vindaloo."* But Nan, it seems, is a Northern province due east of Chiang Mai, towards the Laos border. *"It's where the 'Phi Tong Luang' come from: the Spirits of the Yellow Leaves."* Well that makes it much clearer. He explains that the 'Phi Tong Luang' run around in the jungle, scantily clad, moving home when the leaves of their dwelling turn yellow — hence the name. We arrange to meet the following day in the foyer of Nan's most prestigious hotel — the Dhevaraj. I take a 'tuk–tuk' to Thai Airways and buy my tickets. Spend the night in the Rattana Guest House, just in case.

Thursday, 17th May:
It seems John left yesterday — at round seven pm. He told Rin they were going away on holiday and while she was upstairs packing, he did a runner

in the jeep. Rin, who has now turned to the bottle like many a good Thai, stayed in her room, weeping. Moo, has come back to console her.

She's convinced Rin will soon 'do the deed'.

Flight from Chiang Mai to Nan takes forty minutes on a bumpy Shorts. Search the entire town for John, check every hotel, but no sign of him. I wonder if he's had an accident? Has he suffered the terrible fate he was anticipating? Nan is a dump; there's bugger all to do here. No sign even of the 'Phi Tong Luang'. Not a yellow leaf to be seen.

Friday, 18th May:
Buy the first available return ticket to Chiang Mai. I cannot believe John once described Nan to me as 'really beautiful'. Some of Rin's insanity has rubbed off on him.

Saturday, 19th May:
'Tuk–tuk' from 'geh how' to 'geh how', hoping to remain near the Night Bazaar, but none is suitable. End up at the Lanna Thai, which belies its name: it's grotty. On a nostalgic stroll — making sure I steer well clear of Charoenprathet Soi 6 — I bump into Nissa, a divorcee with a young kid who's one of the few remaining residents of Rin's. Nissa, I think, works as a travel agent but is rarely sober in the evenings. She certainly likes a drink. At one stage I was giving her English tuition until, during a lesson, after explaining to her that I was Jewish, she exclaimed: *"Oh I hate Jews."* I think she was confused between Jews and Israelis; even so it was hardly an auspicious beginning. Term ended shortly after that outburst. Another abortive attempt at teaching. *And* she was sober at the time.

"Where you go?" asks Nissa, as if I'd never been away.

"I go to Nan," I reply in my best broken English. *"What happen to geh how?"* Thai, you see, has no tenses so all communication tends to be done in the present.

"Oh, John and Rin go away together."

"Together? Not possible. John leave Rin. John tell me he go Nan." By now I am completely confused.

So I've been duped. All the way to Nan and not even a glimpse of a 'Phi'. Iew has no doubts: *"John bullshit. All farang bullshit."* A very Thai explanation.

Check out of the Lanna Thai 'geh how' the same afternoon I checked in. The owner, who thinks I'm another 'farang passart', refuses to repay any of my money. *"Money back?"* I inquire optimistically. *"Kaw tohd, kup. Mai dai. Cannot."* Still, the refusal *was* executed with a Thai smile.

Moo's back: poor, misguided woman is still working at Rin's, but living out (maybe not so misguided). The phone rings — it's Rin. They have gone to Chiang Rai. John sounds terrified. He changed his mind and took Rin with him, reckoning it was safer to have the potential assassin by his side rather than far away. Now where's the logic in that? Terror has obviously affected his reasoning. *"They're after me,"* he whispers down the phone.

I can hardly hear what he's saying: after all it is a long distance call from Chiang Rai. *"Who are?"*

"The Kuomintang."

Unwilling on both sides to proceed with this line of discussion, I tut–tut knowingly and replace the receiver.

"What he want John?" asks Iew.

"Mai lu. Farang passart." Succinct . . . and very Thai.

"Farang kee nuk," Iew concludes and wanders off to the Night Bazaar to stock up on some comics. This apparently means 'farang bird shit' and is a common abuse directed at 'farangs' — particularly those who turn up in Bangkok scruffily dressed in just a T–shirt and shorts (the Thais supposedly are very fussy about attire — but not it seems about hurling abuse at 'farangs', despite what you might read in the guide books).

Beware the Kuomintang!

Lying in bed, I remember one evening some days ago when four Thai men came into the guest house and sat drinking Maekhong all night. Now Thais rarely — if ever — came to Rin's. John was immediately suspicious and kept glancing surreptitiously under the table to see if they were armed. It was like a children's pantomime: I half expected someone in the guest house to call out *"behind you, behind you."* I recall John telling me then that they had probably been sent to kidnap him. But they hadn't and they didn't.

Sunday, 20th May:
No sign of anyone yet; pop out to DK Bookshop to buy some guide-books. By the time I've come back, John and Rin will be there and everything will seem just fine. And then I can wake up.

Monday, 21st May:
Poor Korma (the bird) is no more. To test if he could fly, the 'Mad One' released him from his cage (Korma, that is, not John) in the wide–open expanses of Chiang Rai province. *"Flee,"* he chirped, *"flee, flee,"* and he did.

John pays back forty thousand baht and I buy my Hong Kong dollars.

A quiet, pleasant evening is spoilt when Rin finds out about our 'adventure' in Nan. *"Why you go fucking Nan? What you doing?"* And then she storms out.

Tuesday, 22nd May:
Leaving Thailand is not always simple. Or rather: a 'farang's struggle for a Tax Clearance Certificate. This form, given by the local tax office, is necessary for certain foreigners. But no one can tell me which. I must walk into the tax office smiling, say *"Sawatdee kup"* and confess what a beautiful, friendly, smiling country Thailand is. For the woman in the Chiang Mai tax department is well–known with 'farangs' for being a right old sourpuss: yet she was fine with me. I had obviously been sufficiently ingratiating. I hadn't stayed ninety days and so didn't need a certificate.

What she failed to mention was that she herself was not 'au courant' with the Thai tax regulations. My intention was to fly from Chiang Mai to Bangkok, change to the International terminal and go on to Hong Kong. My luggage had already been checked through to my final destination.
 "You have tack mister?" inquired the official.
 "No. Girl in office in Chiang Mai say not need," I reply in my most effective broken English. In the best bureaucratic traditions of South–East Asia, he wanders off to consult his superior, shaking his head.
 "Sorry, cannot leave country. You must pick up bag at Bangkok, take to International terminal, check in again and go to tack office."
 "Tax office. Where that?" I pray it's not downtown, or else I can wave 'largon' to my flight.

It isn't. It's in the airport terminal. I wonder what happened before they had an office there. I apologise profusely, praise beautiful Chiang Mai, admit to not having earned any money and graciously accept a five hundred baht fine with a *"Kop koon kup"*.

First impressions of Hong Kong aren't encouraging: after waiting half an hour for a taxi, I get barged out of the queue by some overweight Chinese man just when it's my turn. I refuse to go to the back of the line and several locals — well, I presume they were locals — start shouting and waving their arms at me. *"Bugger off,"* I reply in my best Cantonese. The taxi driver then rips me off. On checking in at my hotel, I'm greeted with *"And how will you be paying your bill, sir?"* And I've only just arrived. . . oh take me back to the insane normality of Charoenprathet Soi 6.

Friday, 25th May:
After three days in Hong Kong, I am longing for Chiang Mai. Thailand: my rucksack doesn't appear on the luggage belt. *"Mai ben lai, mai ben lai, no problem,"* is the predictable response of the Thai Airways official. Always sodding 'mai ben lai'. *"It may be 'mai ben lai' to you mate, but it's a bloody disaster for me,"* I reply calmly. I must stay calm. I wonder what *doesn't* qualify for a 'mai ben lai' amongst the Thais? John and Rin, who have come to the airport to pick me up, wait patiently and silently.

No luggage ... "mai ben lai".

"You wait neck fly Bangkok. Bag come for sure," the official informs me.
"No problem." Only the lens I bought for John's camera, all my clothes, etc, etc. *"No problem. Mai ben lai. I wait."* Now how could I doubt Thai efficiency? My rucksack arrives one hour later on the next — and final — flight from Bangkok that evening. The customs official is too embarrassed to check the contents. I'm back in Soi 6, relieved.

Tuesday, 29th May:
Things have been very quiet since my return from Hong Kong. Iew has set up a stall outside the 'geh how' selling jewellery he bought in Nakhon Phanom (*"You buy ticket for me for plane. I go home. I buy cheap. I sell good plice — make money too much."*). Did I say 'sell': that's rather a misnomer. He hasn't actually sold anything, but he's quite hopeful even though it's coming to the end of the tourist season. John and Rin appear to be getting on OK — he's branching out into the trekking business and wants me to help. Finally some calm in Chiang Mai.

Wednesday, 30th May:
But not for long: Thomas, a German who ran a restaurant called 'Cockaigne' (which sounds suitably Thai but which according to my dictionary means a legendary land of idleness and luxury — apt indeed for Thailand, but surely wasted on both Thai and 'farang') turns up out of the blue. He's gone bust and is thoroughly disillusioned with the country. He reckons he's blown three hundred thousand baht — his entire savings — and he's split up with his Thai girlfriend. *"She lost interest in the restaurant,"* he explained. *"And worse, the staff kept walking out. The owner of the building gave me a hard time and I had to sell everything. I've lost all my money, so I'm off to Australia. I'll never come back to Thailand. Fucking Thai girls . . ."*

Thursday, 31st May:
John and Rin finally depart on a trip to Nan, on the trail of the 'Yellow Leaves'.

Saturday, 2nd June:
They return, quite cheerful. Moo is leaving after all: and no, I haven't mentioned the loan. John has decided to sell the guest house: customers are thin on the ground. And any that do appear, Rin refuses to serve.

Even her greatest admirer — were he to exist (and that's unlikely) — would have to admit that she wasn't exactly good for business.

Sunday, 3rd June:
Nor is the old drunkard, Nissa. Tonight we had planned to go out, but the sot has left her young son all alone in their shared room. So instead Rin cooks a superb meal — you see she can find other uses for the meat–cleaver when she puts her mind to it (but which one?).

Monday, 4th June:
John is intent on selling the guest house and renting the downstairs for his trekking office, the home of 'Drive Easy Tours'. I suppose that makes sense.

Thai Airways efficiency: my English friend Louise's luggage has arrived at Chiang Mai Airport but hitherto no sign of its proprietor. 'TG' have mislaid her, along with her bags.

Wednesday, 6th June:
Two days late (*"Engine trouble at Heathrow, engine failure over North Sea, TG"*), Louise appears, and familiarises herself again with her luggage waiting at Rin's. I immediately warn her against engaging in any sort of conversation with John: unless, of course, she wants to come face to face with a range of Thai kitchen utensils.

John has discovered a superb restaurant just outside Chiang Mai. The food is authentic, the singing entertaining and the dancing . . . well, that can only be described as extraordinary. The girls are always out of time — or those that move are. Most simply wiggle their backsides, glued to the spot. Another fine meal was marred, not by Rin this time but by a Thai man beating up his wife in the car–park. Rin explained that it was to do with a minor or major wife — I couldn't understand which, or why for that matter. Something about one wife catching her husband out with the other wife. John wanted to intervene as the husband kept bashing the poor girl's head up against the window of his car, but Iew stopped him: *"Not my cousin,"* he said. *"Not my cousin."*

Thursday, 7th June:
Another skirmish in the 'War of the Orchids' is imminent.

Friday, 8th June:
Rin insane today. I must check the psychiatrists's section of Chiang Mai's 'Yellow Pages'.

Saturday, 9th June:
John and I have been busy organising the trek — the guinea pig for 'Drive Easy Tours'. Rin refuses to have anything to do with it: in the end, she decides to come — no doubt to keep an eye on John. I tell him I don't want her spoiling everything with her moods. So she sulks and sits in the front of the minibus, miffed.

Now Thai drivers are notoriously bad — their motto's simple: if it moves overtake it. And if it's heading towards you on the same side of the road (as the Thais tend to do after a couple of swigs of Maekhong), wait till the very last moment and then swerve violently to avoid it. That should shake the passengers up a bit. The road accident statistics make grim reading: over two hundred killed each month. And we've got ourselves a 'traditional' Thai driver.

We head north from Chiang Mai on the road to Chiang Rai, the ugly town used as a base for many treks. We stop off near Mae Suai (which strangely enough means either 'beautiful' or 'unlucky mother' according to the tone. Strange language — much to Iew and Rin's amusement I coined the Thai phrase 'bpaat pet ped'; if pronounced quickly the words practically sound the same. It actually means 'eight spicy ducks' in Thai) south west of Chiang Rai. We have discovered a resort — called Charin Garden — where tourists are accommodated in quaint little bungalows by a river. There are all sorts of animals, too — and, naturally, elephants to appease the 'farangs'.

The Akha village we visit is one rarely seen by tourists and the children come running out to see us: they are as bemused as Louise. They stare, coy and timid, unsure what to make of us outsiders. They are particularly fascinated by John's binoculars and, though reticent at first, take turns in peering through the eye–pieces. They can't quite comprehend what they're seeing. The rest of the group gets stoned on dope which they've been offered. I resist, though with our driver in the mood he's in, it may not have been such a bad idea after all.

On our way back we pass through a Lisu village, which John and I first discovered on our trip a month ago. We stop and wander about, but Rin is decidedly edgy and stays in the minibus. I wrongly assume she's in another one of her moods. John has discovered a helipad on the village school-games pitch, and his suspicions are confirmed when the headman — a Fu Manchu-type character with a goatee beard — appears. John orders us swiftly back into the minibus. A Lisu village with a Chinese headman means only one thing — opium. We depart hastily. *"You lucky this time,"* says Rin. *"Too dangerous. Next time maybe Lisu kill farang."* For once, she was having a moment of lucidity.

Sunday, 10th June:
Leave Mae Suai and head north, returning once again to the 'Golden Triangle' and to Mae Sai. We have planned to spend the night in a Yao village — uninvited, of course — which is reached by means of a slippery mountain road. By now, however, the mad Thai driver had ensured there was no tread left on the tyres, and with the recent rains reducing the track to little more than a muddy piste, the minibus — inconveniently rear–wheel drive — came to a grinding halt. We all get out to assess the situation: the driver is convinced he can make it and keeps revving up the engine. But the wheels, as if on some Alpine skating rink, just spin round and round. It's time to push lads. I feel sorry for my guests, but we've no choice. Two tribesmen, on their way home from working in the fields and both armed with rifles — join us. We can't communicate, but who needs language when our plight is obvious. John, in fact, is still working on his hilltribe phrasebook, but alas expressions like *"Excuse me my good man you couldn't just give us a helping hand with our minibus?"* aren't included.

Progress is slow: the drizzle continues and dusk is almost upon us. With a plastic bag over her head to shield her from the rain — and at the same time reminiscent of some creature out of a Peter Cushing movie — Rin attempts to solve the problem her way. She rips some fern from the shrubbery nearby and places it under the tyres: this, according to her, will enable the wheels to go round. We look on with amazement: not because her dotty plan succeeds, but astounded by the madness behind it. At long last, after much shoving and swearing, the minibus advances and to a loud cheer we are back on our way. The tyres, however, are in need of urgent attention.

We are warmly received in the village. The headman, who speaks Thai, welcomes us and soon hordes of curious children come to gawp at us. Who, I wonder, is the more fascinated? *"Moi ming hai,"* says John in his best Yao. This should mean *"hello"* but the response is merely one of astonishment.

We have brought our own food which Rin and Iew cook in the headman's house, assisted by some of the Yao women. The Yao, also known as Mien, originally came from Southern China over two hundred years ago. They migrated through Laos and into Thailand where they number now around forty thousand, with many more in China and Vietnam. They are amongst the friendliest and most hospitable of all the hilltribes. And we certainly saw testimony of that.

The headman allocated us our accommodation: we were given three houses whose owners didn't appear to have any say in the matter. What the headman said, went. But they all seemed honoured to put us up. My house was smoky — they had a fire by the bedside — which smouldered all night. I must have been lodged in the 'wing' near the pigsty as the grunting kept me awake, as did the incessant rain. So I rose early to a cool, dank morning and wandered outside. The lady of the house was busy preparing our meal, chopping bamboo on the floor. After breakfast, we were on our way.

The driver changed the tyre as we set out towards Doi Mae Salong. With spectacular views of the Burmese hills, Doi Mae Salong is very much a Chinese town. Most of the inhabitants are Chinese refugees — known as Kuomintang (now that rings a bell) — from the Communist revolution of 1949. At the roadside stalls you can purchase all kinds of weird drinks and potions: liquors with snakes floating in them and rare whiskies.

On our way home we pass through Thaton, near the Burmese border and on to Chiang Dao with its mountain and caves beneath. It has been a tiring day and it is good to be able to have a warm shower. But before we can all retire peacefully to bed, Rin says she's leaving and gets drunk. She disappears to Cheddar's bar: Rin's friend Cheddar (I doubt that's the correct spelling) ran a bar where the 'Mad One' often sought refuge. This would invariably give John something to joke about in his moments of anguish: *"So she's gone to Cheddar's bar, has she?"* he'd say. *"She must be really cheesed off."* *"Ah yes,"* he'd continue, *"Cheddar's the gorgeous one you know?"* Droll? Well it certainly eased the tension.
　　The perfect end to a perfect day.

Tuesday, 12th June:
I've finally decided to move on from Chiang Mai. The guest house is crumbling around me.

Wednesday, 13th June:
The seventy-seven day nightmare is over. Iew has sold everything he can't take with him (the next door neighbour has secured the TV amongst many other bargains) and we sneak out to breakfast with Louise at the Pornping Hotel. I can relax at last, and look forward to Phuket again.

Friday, 15th June:
I have five days in Phuket, before flying on to Ko Samui. I want to relax and forget the mad turmoil, the hysteria of Chiang Mai but am filled with confusion and compunction: was I right to leave so suddenly, what wreckage lies in my wake? My three months, I suppose, were quite unexceptional by Chiang Mai standards, merely a microcosm of Northern Thai society, of Thai/'farang' relationships. My God, what a life, what an endurance.

Monday, 18th June:
So, welcome instead to Ko Samui International Airport: not 'International' quite yet, perhaps, but how long to wait? Iew, not fully acquainted with seatbelts, is hurtled upwards as the miniscule Boeing Dash 8 of Bangkok Airways encounters Don Muang–style turbulence shortly before touchdown.

Tuesday, 19th June:
Ko Samui: coconut fringed palms, clean, blue waters: everything the travel brochures say. And less hassle than Phuket (at the moment). Yes the fake gem dealers pester you, but on the whole it's more relaxed. Soon an American girl, right in front of me, will fall for the well rehearsed 'looby from Burma' routine. I feel I should warn her, but the Thai trader, of brutish appearance, would no doubt take exception to this 'farang' interfering: so instead I use the Thai approach for once and mumble *"not my cousin"* convincingly to myself. In any case, if it's gems she wants she should go to Bangkok. For the capital has the best diamonds money can buy . . . directly from at least two police generals. How jealous De Beers would be: if only they knew.

Thursday, 21st June:
Iew attempts water–skiing. Two hundred baht's worth of unqualified disaster. Both times he went aquaplaning rather than skiing. And in typical Thai fashion the boat driver wouldn't give us our money back. I argued that Iew hadn't actually water–skied: he'd spent five abortive minutes attempting to do so.

"You give money back?" I inquired hopefully.

He pretended not to understand, yet not ten minutes ago his English had come quite readily. Well he knew how to screw two hundred baht out of a gullible 'farang'. No refund, no charm, no smiling face.

Monday, 25th June:
Bangkok is beckoning. I've run out of travellers cheques and I'm running out of patience. I'm ready to return home; I could do with a holiday.

Bangkok Airways Dash 8 wings us back to 'Krung Thep'. Not wishing to come face to antennae again with the Miami Hotel cockroaches, I select the Golden Gate Hotel, right at the beginning of Sukhumvit, on Soi 2. I've picked the hotel from an ad in the magazine 'Thaiways': one night with full American breakfast is priced at five hundred baht — the ad goes on : 'with no hidden extras for our guests'. Sounds good value. I check in.

"You have room?"

"Yes sir."

"Five hundred baht a night?" I ask.

"No sir, five hundred and fifty baht," the receptionist replies, feigning surprise. I show her the ad. *"Five hundred baht you see. No hidden extras."*

"Sorry sir, cannot do for five hundred baht. Five hundred baht plus ten per cent tack. Five hundred and fifty."

No hidden extras — except for ten per cent, of course. But executed with centuries old Thai charm.

Tuesday, 26th June:
I have a few days before leaving for the UK. Make the most of the time to spend money, deftly avoiding all touts and all Thais who offer me a *"special plice"* for anything. At times I'd like to feel lonely in this frenetic 'City of Angels'.

Buy ten metres of four ply silk from one of the numerous Indian–run silk shops on Sukhumvit. I knock the price down to two thousand eight hundred baht. Later I'm reliably informed that I've paid too little for the silk and it must be fake. Fake? Apparently they mix the silk with plastic synthetics — a common ruse in Bangkok. In spite of everything, I'm just another gullible 'farang' after all.

Wednesday, 27th June:
"Mai ben lai, mai ben lai," I say slowly to myself. I've asked the taxi driver to take me to the Tax Clearance Office — remember that from Chiang Mai? He doesn't appear to comprehend. In desperation I get out my passport and point to the page containing the Thai visa. *"Tax, tax. Stay long time,"* I repeat. Suddenly he seems to have got the message. He puts his foot down. Twenty minutes later I am standing in the queue at the Immigration Office. I show him my passport. He shakes his head.
    "Why you come here?" he inquires.
    "I must get Tax Certificate." I reply respectfully, wondering why he's asked such an obvious question.
    "Not here. At Tack Office," he asserts peremptorily.
    "Tax Office? This is *the Tax Office."*
    "This is Immigration Office. Khon dtor bai kup."
    "Mai ben lai, kup."
    I leave in search of a 'tuk–tuk'. But none will take me: *"Too far. Too many car. Take too long time."* Sometimes you just want to scream . . but then that's taboo in the 'Land of Smiles'.

Thursday, 28th June:
The genuine (if anything in Thailand *is* genuine) Tax Office is my first real taste of Bangkok bureaucracy. I can't understand a word they're saying. I'm given a card with a number on it and I assume I have to wait until that number is called. But seeing as all the announcements are given out in Thai, how on earth am I going to know when it's my turn? I appear to be the only 'farang' waiting. So every time a number is called, I go up to the desk only to be greeted with a gruff shaking of the head. What else can I do? Learn my Thai numerals, I suppose. *"Nung, song, sahm, si, hah, hok, jet, bpaat, gao, sip . . ."* I knew my phrase book would come in handy one day. After all, at least this time the 'tuk–tuk' driver understood when I said *"I go office tack. Pah–see."*

An hour or so later I'm sitting in front of a young female Thai tax official. She looks through my passport.

"You stay in Thailand long time. Where you get money to stay long time?" she inquires.

"I have travellers cheques and credit cards. And I open bank account and have money sent from England." I show her my Thai Farmers Bank passbook.

"Why you stay long time? You work in Thailand?"

This is the cue for my well rehearsed response. *"Thailand very beautiful. People very friendly. I want to see country. Travel everywhere. Where you come from? You like football?"* That last bit was thrown in because the World Cup was in full swing and the Thais were all football–crazy. I was frantically trying to divert her attention from my financial affairs. Absurd thoughts flashed through my mind: what if Rin had told her I'd once bought part of the guest house: What if . . .

"No. I like tennis," she replied.

"Ah, Wimbledon. I live near Wimbledon . . ."

She stamps my passport and issues my Tax Certificate. *"Next time you pay tack."* In my best Thai I thank her and bid her good day. You see what you get with flattery and a smiling face . . .

I left Don Muang International Airport, Bangkok, on Sunday, July 15th. I passed through Passport Control with no problems. To my great chagrin the official didn't seem at all interested in my Tax Clearance Certificate. It must have been the beaming smile I gave him as I handed over my documents . . .

PART TWO

VIETNAM AND BURMA

Twelve weeks later I was back in Bangkok, weaving my way through the traffic to the Golden Gate Hotel, Sukhumvit Soi 2.

Tuesday, 9th October:
Of all the countries in South–East Asia, Burma holds the greatest mystique for me. The very names conjure up wonderful images: Pagan, Mandalay, the Irrawaddy. Alas my visa application is rejected by the Burmese Embassy in Bangkok: my former profession (as described in my passport) of 'Racing journalist' debars me from entering this politically sensitive country.

I had been following the political activities in Burma — or Myanmar as the authorities have now renamed it — since the elections of May 27th this year. Burma has always seemed the most complex of nations — a country permanently divided by a conflict of interests. Who was it who once said: 'Put two Burmese together and you'll have an argument' (or words to that effect)? Even by the standards of its stormy past, Burma, with its myriad of ethnic groups, was enduring harsh times. And journalists, for sure, of whatever description were not welcome. I was told the story of a genuine visitor who was refused entry at Rangoon's Mingaladon Airport because it said 'geologist' in his passport. The official couldn't differentiate apparently between journalist and geologist.

So it was to Vietnam, instead, that I turned my attention. Unlike Burma, which appears to be reversing swiftly both politically and economically, Vietnam is attempting to progress. This much beleaguered nation is finally opening its doors again to the world, though the way ahead is a long and arduous one.

Due to its isolation from the West, few airlines fly from Bangkok to Ho Chi Minh's Tan Son Nhat airport, the choice being realistically limited to Thai Airways or Air France. For obvious reasons, travel agents are desperate to encourage tourists to fly on Hang Khong Vietnam. Now no one in their right mind flies with *them*, well, no one except the poor Vietnamese. For Hang Khong's safety record — or rather lack of — is surpassed only by that of Burma Airways Corporation.

"You fly with Vietnam, you go very soon," the girl in the travel agency proudly asserted.

"Yes, and no come back" I replied. She looked at me blankly and mumbled *"arai?"* to her colleague who was seated next to her. The colleague had clearly understood and giggled. *"You go Air Flance, cannot go before October 25."* She was doing a masterly job for Hang Khong's PR. But it was an unequal struggle.

"OK, mai ben lai. I get you Air Flance." The immediate problem then: where to go now? Vientiane on Lao Aviation, Phnom Penh on Kampuchean Airlines? No, Seoul on Delta. *"Why you go Corear?"* asks Iew bemused. I give him my best Thai response: *"Up to me."*

Friday, 12th October:
About to check in for my flight to South Korea and no Tax Clearance Certificate. I'm completely confused again: it all depends, so they say, on whether you have a Tourist or a Non–immigrant visa, and whether you stay more than fifteen days — or was it ninety? Well, nothing can be done now. It's five am and the office is shut. Keep smiling.

Stopover in Taipei, and then on to Kimpo Airport, Seoul. Iew, leaving his country for the first time (he wouldn't even cross the border at Mae Sai for a few moments), is quite bemused. But it all seems like home when the taxi driver rips us off: and that despite the meter working perfectly. For some reason he demanded a supplement, and my Korean wasn't up to answering back. Goodbye to my pile of won.

For Iew, Seoul is cold. It is a modern, busy, bustling city. It reminds me of Hong Kong. Some say the traffic here rivals Bangkok, but that's nonsense. There are few 'farangs'.

Sunday, 14th October:
It's a wonderful, crisp autumn day as we visit the Changdok Palace, the Secret Garden, the Skyway and — Thai–style — an amethyst factory. I didn't know South Korea was famous for its amethysts: but the prices they charge in the factory would make a Bangkok jeweller blush with shame.

Monday, 15th October:
Extraordinary quantities and weird types of mushrooms are on sale at the market: it's a vast place. Iew is goggle–eyed: he wants to buy everything. The Koreans are rather shy and timid, without the outgoing friendliness of many of the South–East Asian nations. And the food . . . 'mai aloy'. It's vinegary and there's little variety. Poor Iew, away from his homeland for the first time, is quite put out. Each restaurant we visit, he asks plaintively: *"Have tom yam?"* Alas no, so we eat at the expensive Western restaurants in the vast Lotte Hotel complex: Iew cheers up when he sees the size of the bill.

Wednesday, 17th October:
We leave today. Iew keeps saying he wants to see a film: I explain that they don't have Thai movies here, he simply replies *"mai ben lai."* So we end up seeing *Emanuelle IV* in French with Korean subtitles. He can't understand a word — and the sex scenes are heavily edited. The Koreans seem quite a prudish race. I understand French but the sound quality is so poor that I am unable to make out most of the dialogue. Not that the text is of much significance: the film consists of various sexual encounters, mainly of a lesbian nature. We leave at half–time to catch our flight back to Bangkok.

Thursday, 18th October:
Inch'on at night is an interesting spot, though I'd rather be in Bangkok. Shortly before our departure, an announcement came: *"Due to passenger being taken ill, Delta flight to Bangkok via Taipei cancelled. Thank you and goodnight."* Apparently the plane had to make a 'mercy' landing in Tokyo and, because Kimpo shuts at around ten o'clock at night — not bad for a so–called international airport — it was good night to Delta customers. This delay, of course, causes consternation and frustration: everyone jostling around the Delta desk. The poor representative, who can barely speak English, is harassed. *"I must be in Bangkok tomorrow morning", "I have a business meeting in Taipei,"* and so on. They all had their excuses: as for me, well I didn't want to be left out of it. *"I have an important conference to attend in Bangkok early tomorrow afternoon. You must find me a seat on the first available flight."* But for the time being, it was off by bus to the New Star Hotel, all expenses paid and free long–distance calls to England.

Wisely, Iew and I teamed up with a Singaporean pharmacologist, who *was* on his way to Bangkok for a meeting, and (maybe not so wisely) an American marine based in South Korea who was off to meet his Thai wife near Bangkok. This was to be his first trip to the Kingdom. He was everything you'd expect a US marine to be: tall, broad and very stupid. The Singaporean, too, was something of a caricature. He was frighteningly efficient and spent his time organising everyone and everything. Iew thought it was just 'sanuk'. *"Flee, flee?"* he kept inquiring. *"Yes,"* I said, *"everything flee."*

We were told to be up at six o'clock, though no one knew what flight they'd be on. At five minutes to six, the Singaporean was up, shaved, showered and packed and waiting impatiently for his breakfast. With him at the helm, we couldn't go far wrong. After all, he *did* have a meeting to attend.

Kimpo Airport is a madhouse. I sit waiting while the others form a rugby scrum around the Delta desk. The options appear to be: wait for yesterday's cancelled flight which is scheduled to leave at six o'clock in the evening —

i.e. hang about all day in the airport — and judging by the frowns, that isn't a popular choice. Or be re–routed on Thai, Cathay Pacific (via Hong Kong) or Singapore (via Taipei and Singapore). Our Singaporean is travelling business class and making such a nuisance of himself, that he's the first to go — on Thai. The US marine, Iew and I just wait. The marine is very worried: his few days of leave are slipping away (so he feels) and he's worried what he should do when he reaches Bangkok. His wife comes from Ratchaburi — south–west of the capital — and Iew, in his best broken English, is trying to advise him. The marine, though based in Korea, has little experience of how Orientals communicate in English, whilst Iew cannot follow his constant *"Jeez, man"* and similar Americanisms. *"Your friend,"* he asks. *"He speaks English, man?"* *"Sort of,"* I reply. *"Jeez, I can't understand a God–damn word."* *"What he say?"* inquires Iew. Oh at times like this it's just impossible whatever the nationality.

East meets West.

The Delta representative has been working like . . . well, like a Singaporean, and for little credit. Where there were no seats on Singapore Airlines, seats have miraculously appeared (a very Asian trait) and we are told to hurry to the departure lounge. *"Now I hope you make your meeting in Bangkok sir. Thank you for flying Delta."* Delta?

"Meeting you where?" asks Iew in typical Thai reverse order. *"Farang bullshit again. Always bullshit. Me, I not worry. Everything flee."*

Bangkok. The marine is completely baffled. It is a terrible city to arrive in, alone, tired and confused. And in the stifling heat you are easy prey for the touts. I said goodbye as he was trying to escape from a man pestering him with *"Mister you want taxi na? Massage? Lady? Boy?"*

Saturday, 20th October:
I have moved to Suriwong Road, in the heart of the smog, stench and pollution that are Patpong. Who on earth do Thai hoteliers get to translate their menus into English, and why don't they check the extraordinary results? The choices don't match up to the 'king crap in pot' at Chiang Mai's bizarre restaurant, but still there's 'magafonic soup', 'scrambied on toast', 'magaronid salad' and 'fried noodles and sauce with bees'. *"Aloy na kup?"*.

Monday, 22nd October:
Collecting my visas and tickets for Vietnam, I notice, by chance, a brochure advertising new trips to Burma — cultural tours, organised by a company called Lanna Air Tours. These trips are the brainchild of a Burmese–speaking French tour operator named Geneviève Goux who, after months of trying, has finally received permission from the Burmese authorities to fly from Chiang Mai to Pagan, on to Mandalay and back to Chiang Mai. And *not* with Burma Air, but with Thailand's domestic carrier Bangkok Airways. Bangkok Airways have been in business for twenty years, but the Thai government, anxious to protect the monopoly of the state–owned Thai Airways International, only permits them to fly selected routes — mainly unfashionable ones. But recently they acquired the rights to Ko Samui — and that is one over the Thai government.

This could be the only way into Burma for me: for, to quote the brochure — 'visa issue on arrival in Pagan'. I shall keep my former profession quiet until departure and see what happens. Apparently this is only the second group in: very much 'farang' guinea pigs.

Tuesday, 23rd October:
'Tuk–tuk' to Oriental Hotel pier — I've still to enter the place, which isn't so grand from the outside. I remember a tale a girl told me. She was arriving in Bangkok from Sydney and had booked one night at the Oriental. She turned up late at night, exhausted and clad solely in T–shirt and shorts. Despite having a reservation, she was turfed out because of her 'scruffy' appearance; they didn't care that she had just spent several hours on a plane. So she took a taxi to the Shangri–La: there they welcomed her, offered her a superb room and prepared supper for her: and that despite the fact that she had no reservation and it was past midnight. Who said the Oriental was the best hotel in the world?

Anyway, just an outside glimpse of the place as we take the river boat up the Chao Phya River to Wat Po. This is my third visit to the temple of the Reclining Buddha and it never ceases to impress. Massage here — of the traditional (i.e. non sexual) Thai type — is wonderful, but only if you don't mind a bit of pain. Oh Bangkok would be a near flawless city if it weren't for the heat, the pollution and . . the traffic. You just can't escape it. Silom and Suriwong Roads are particularly bad: at the intersection with Rama 4 Road, I once waited twelve minutes for the lights to change. And then it's a mad, frenetic scramble with exhaust fumes clouding out of the buses and cars, motorbikes weaving about desperately and 'tuk–tuks' tooting their horns interminably. It's a crazy place. But what about Patpong?

Ah Patpong, Patpong, it has to be seen to be believed: the place has an extraordinary buzz to it, almost tangible. In the day, the two 'sois' are non-descript, just streets with shops, bars and restaurants. But at night it comes alive as the touts and vendors move in and the hordes of 'farangs' descend. It's pushy, animated and vital: poor, uneducated girls from 'Isaan', in search of their fortune, out to trap a hapless 'farang'. He, in turn, is out for easy sex and no commitment. But how many are ensnared by the sly cunning and guile of the bar–girl? One night in Bangkok, that could just last forever.

On one of the 'sois' near Patpong is the Rome Club, the coolest disco in town. Thais like to be cool, to be admired; they're so incredibly vain. The Rome Club is packed every night with all types: boys, girls and what the Thais call 'kateuys' or 'ladyboys'. Often it's impossible to tell a 'kateuy' from a girl, for in Thailand, all is not as it seems. There is the story of a 'farang' in Pattaya who struck up conversation with a Thai 'lady'. Now the 'lady' was keen for the liaison to go a little further and somehow lured the naive 'farang' into her boudoir. Shocked and horrified, the 'farang' turned down the advances with the desperate plea *"Sorry I can't stay, you see I'm gay. I don't go with girls."* *"No problem"* replied the 'lady' who then ripped off 'her' wig, removed 'her' boobs and dropped 'her' skirt to reveal 'her' manhood. Needless to say, the 'farang' fled the scene in terror. The highlight at the Rome Club is the nightly 'kateuy' show — or 'Cabaret' as the Thais call it. It's very camp, very amateurish but very entertaining as some Thai boy kitted out like Shirley Bassey mimes out of time to *Hey Big Spender.* The Thais love it. On this night I was talking to one of the waiters (from Chiang Mai) about my travel plans, when his eyes suddenly lit up and he announced: *"So you are a missionary?"* For once I was too aston-ished to reply.

Thursday, 25th October:
It seems rather incongruous touching down at Tan Son Nhat Airport, Ho Chi Minh in this vast Boeing 747 of Air France. We glide gracefully past the pitiful Tupolevs of Hang Khong Vietnam on a runway that is crying out for resurfacing. Hordes of hopeful touts and taxi–drivers — plus the merely curious — greet the twice weekly arrival of the Air France Jumbo. But before you can get anywhere near them, you have to subject yourself to Vietnamese bureaucracy: Immigration and Customs. Tan Son Nhat just

wasn't built to cope with this many passengers. You go from queue to queue, official to official, clutching your forms in your by now sweaty palms (naturally there's no air conditioning, only ineffective fans). You are asked to declare all currency and valuables: and then they search *everything*. It's infuriating, it's disorganised, it's Vietnam.

Our guide from Saigontourist, a charming man named Nguyen Ngoc Sang (numerous Vietnamese are called 'Nguyen', however it's pronounced), is on hand to welcome us. His English is remarkable, particularly in view of the shortage of English books in Saigon. He's remarkably well read, too, and repeatedly quotes from Conrad and Somerset Maugham. I feel ashamed by my ignorance.

The drive to the hotel is quite unlike anything I've ever experienced. Instead of 'tuk–tuks', there are bicycles, everywhere, hovering like Thais round a 'farang'. And yes, girls wearing conical hats.

The names may have changed, but the character hasn't (well, except for the Australian arrival, the Saigon Floating Hotel, that is). The Caravelle has become the Doc Lap, still in dire need of renovation and with outrageous rates (in the region of fifty US dollars), but it's got style: not least the restaurant on the top floor with its unrivalled panorama of Saigon — and terrific breakfast. And there's no doubt: Vietnamese cuisine is streets ahead of Korean: bypass the ubiquitous 'cha gio' (spring rolls), for there are exquisite dishes like 'chao tom' — shrimps with sugar cane.

After supper we take a stroll outside the hotel, and are taken aback by the battalion of kids, beggars it seems, who pester us the moment we set foot on the street. It appears to be a well organised ring of waifs, or is it that I'm too cynical? Certainly in Chiang Mai, there were groups of Thai 'Oliver Twists' — the more winsome the better — sent on their begging ways by racketeering Thai elders. And what sympathy (and baht) the kids elicited. But who knows: Vietnam, after all, is so much poorer than Thailand. The children are so persistent, yet if you give to one, the rest will become even pushier.

And then there are the cyclo riders and the touts and the vendors offering matches, chewing gum, old Vietnamese stamps and drawings . . . it's a never ending list, I feel uneasy, but this is Saigon.

A sad contrast: we while away the evening drinking Saigon Export in the bar. Was it ever like this for Graham Greene?

Friday, 26th October:
After an early breakfast, we set off for the Zoo. Our delightful guide is full of chatter: he earns, so he tells me, roughly thirty dollars a month, a good

wage by Saigon standards. There are no luxuries, so he'd be grateful if I could send him some books — if that was all right — when I got home. First he'd like *The Forsyte Saga*, and then maybe some Somerset Maugham — oh yes, and also *The Satanic Verses*, he'd heard all about that one. But no, not Conrad, thanks, he'd read them all.

In Saigon, cars aren't the worry when you cross the road, it's bikes, bikes everywhere. And beggars, so many beggars, and lepers, crippled, aimless. Some faces I can't forget . . . there's just no life in their eyes, so helpless. I try to give to the lepers: one thousand, two thousand, five thousand dong. Only notes, for there are no coins; and with the highest denomination five thousand — less than a dollar — you'd best bring a wheel–barrow if you're changing large amounts. But I suspect they're all happy with dollars.

The Zoo, situated by a beautiful lake, is entertaining if a little in decline. By the main gate is the History Museum, and our guide embarks on a long tale about Vietnamese history. Iew is more interested in buying an ice–cream and wanders off. Alone, the guide and I return to a favourite topic: the merits of Maupassant and Flaubert and other nineteenth century French literary masters. Why bother about the War?

I stop off at a lacquerware shop, one of the predominant businesses, it seems, in Saigon. I buy two boxes: the prices are so cheap I am ashamed to haggle. But you must, so I pay less than a dollar for two delightful boxes. I leave feeling guilty but with a 'cam on nhieu' — the only words of Vietnamese I know.

Saturday, 27th October:
The Cu Chi Tunnels — in Cu Chi district, about two hours drive from Ho Chi Minh — are on most tourists' agenda. Not being at all interested in the War, I was reluctant to go, but had no choice. It's a shame if Vietnam is only remembered for the War: the country offers much more than that. It was a fascinating journey, an evocative drive through Greater Ho Chi Minh City. I would love to have stopped every few minutes for a closer look at the men at work in the ricefields. And the women, too, all pulling together. I wondered how they managed to look so graceful in the heat. Perhaps it was the protection offered by their conical hats. Now surely that's the image — along with the paddy–fields — which we in the West should associate with Vietnam and its countryside.

The vast network of tunnels — over two hundred kilometres in all — enabled the Viet Cong to evade the Imperialist invaders. They are an extraordinary achievement: meeting rooms, living quarters, all much deeper under the ground than you could possibly have imagined. Before descending, we are given a lecture on the tunnels and shown an old war video. How bizarre to see a video machine here, let alone one that works.

Well 'functions' is maybe a better word: it barely worked. The quality of the tape, too, was ropy. But Iew and I sat glued to our benches as the bombs rained down. Most of the tunnels were eventually destroyed by the Americans, but, by then, they had served their purpose. The Vietnamese are justifiably proud of the Cu Chi Tunnels.

The time had come for us to explore. We set off into the jungle, and then stopped at the chosen spot. The guide asked me to find the entrance to a tunnel: I couldn't see one. He smiled, then rubbed away the mud and leaves with his foot. And there it was, ingeniously camouflaged. We walked on. With the aid of a torch we descended into one of the tunnels: immediately a bat, disturbed by the sound of footsteps, flew out past my ears. Now bats aren't my favourite creatures: so I declined, rather chicken–hearted, to go any further. I sat on a tree stump near the entrance, all now completely tranquil and waited for the others to return.

I bought drinks for our guides and we took shade nearby. Nguyen Ngoc Sang spoke marvellous English, but our driver barely a word. Now the following day we were going to Vung Tau, a coastal resort about two hours from Ho Chi Minh, recommended by a charming Vietnamese lady who had sat next to me on the flight from Bangkok. Saigontourist — acting under instructions from the government — insisted that tourists be accompanied by a guide on all trips outside Ho Chi Minh. And, they expected you not only to pay for hiring the guide (at a wildly inflated price), but also to fork out for their accommodation. Still at least the driver spoke English — or so we were assured by Saigontourist.

Perhaps they should have said *"speaks (very) limited (broken) English,"* for he kept calling me 'Niss' (for Nick) which, from a distance, sounded rather like 'Miss'. *"Niss, Niss,"* he would yell and I would pretend not to understand, merely shrug my shoulders at passers–by. The name 'Iew' has confused many a more fluent English speaker than our Vietnamese driver, so *he* couldn't comprehend at all what 'Iew' meant or how it should be used. So we ended up as 'Niss' and 'hey you' — the sum total of his English phrases — save for a rather curious expression. *"Tonight, happee nice"* with the word 'happee' being rather drawn out. Communication thus consisted of the somewhat repetitive and meaningless *"Niss, tonight happee nice,"* which I presume was Saigon–speak for: *"Nick, have a happy night tonight."*

Later that day, I took a cyclo to the Lao Consulate in search of a visa but it was closed, so instead I asked the driver to take me to the Ben Thanh Market, a rather sad place with beggars and lepers everywhere. They are, I suppose, an inevitable part of Saigon — and indeed Vietnamese — society: the West doesn't know how lucky it is. I then get caught in one of the most vicious downpours I've witnessed — fortunately the cyclo drivers have covers to protect the helpless passengers. But the cover leaks and I get a thorough drenching. 'Songkran', Saigon-style.

Sunday, 28th October:
The French called Vung Tau 'Cap Saint Jacques', a name which conjures up images of Nice and the Côte d'Azur — but don't be misled. A two hour car–ride south–east of Ho Chi Minh City, Vung Tau is more Cleethorpes than Cannes. It is also the base of a Soviet company operating off–shore oil–rigs. And what I hoped might have been a pleasant journey is marred by the driver's apparent obsession with the 'Lambada' — or to be more precise with the one and only cassette he had in his car. No sooner had one side finished than he turned the cassette over. And so on . . . until Vung Tau.

In Vung Tau, and throughout Vietnam, booking a room is a complicated affair. The procedure is this: firstly you have to choose your hotel and check with the driver that it's government approved. Then he has to ask the receptionist whether she accepts tourists (and if he'll get his ten per cent) and then, finally, if they actually *have* any rooms. What luck, the Hai Au Hotel even has its own 'private beach'. Better described as a minute, dirty strip of sand. The sea was filthy: Iew refused point–blank to go near it. *"Sockapock"* was all he'd say. The hotel has a large sign outside advertising its 'new fishing boat': I inquired about the boat and a possible fishing trip but was told *"Sorry, boat not finish yet. Fishing not possible."* Well we certainly weren't going to get much sunbathing or swimming done. . . . But, I'm forgetting, the hotel had its own swimming pool, and just outside my bedroom too. Alas, it appeared to be full of murky sea–water. *"I can swim in pool?"* I ask the receptionist. *"Sorry, sir. Swimming pool not finish. Sea very good . . ."*

I have already paid one hundred and thirty dollars for the guide to accompany us, and on checking in, was surprised to see him inquiring about a room for himself (at thirty dollars). I didn't wish to appear mean, but on the other hand didn't wish to fork out ninety dollars for his accommodation in Vung Tau's most expensive hotel. So I asked the receptionist, who spoke passable English. *"He have friend in town. He stay with friend."* She assured me. Well that's saved me fifty quid.

Monday, 29th October:
Change money on the black market — which is scarcely better than the official rate. Still it saves the hassle of hanging around in the bank.

The beaches may be unattractive, the countryside and scenery are anything but. There are the fishermen working on the shore, unloading their catch and drying their nets; fascinating temples and a huge figure of Jesus overlooking the sea. But above all it is the people: their warmth, their friendliness, their soft, gentle nature and their modesty. They make it all worthwhile.

At Vung Tau market, the girls — so timid and meek at first — smile and blush, particularly when I ask to take their photo. It is easy to see why Westerners lose their heart to Oriental girls — and the Vietnamese are so graceful. And, as my massage that evening was to prove, dogged and determined.

I had learnt that, unlike in Thailand where 'massage' was little more than a euphemism for 'nookie', in Vietnam it most certainly was not. A hostess at a dance, for example, was simply a companion — nothing more. Caressing and groping were taboo: after the dance, you said your good–byes and parted — alone. With this in mind, I was quite looking forward to my Vietnamese massage, blissfully unaware of Vung Tau's reputation as the 'Bangkok' of Vietnam. My masseuse was well past her prime, plain, you would have to say.

    "Everything off," she commanded.
    "Pardon?" I inquired, rather taken aback.
    "Your clothe off. Everything off, take shower and come here," she said, pointing to the bed.
    "Have shower but not take off clothes," I stated firmly and marched off to the bathroom.

A Vietnamese spring roll?

On my return, the masseuse was waiting for me with a mischievous grin on her face. I kept a firm grip of the towel round my waist and lay down on the bed. *"Take away towel,"* she ordered.

"Cannot."

"Why? You not want massage?"

How could I explain. I wanted a 'traditional' massage, nothing more, and certainly not with her. I was English. The English were very shy. She giggled. But I kept the towel on, despite her constantly trying to work and wriggle her hands up to my groin. Time and again I would be forced to fend off her advances. Against such determination, she finally gave in. The only 'dong' she got her mitts on was the wad I handed over at the end. She smiled and said *"You come again?"* *"Maybe,"* I replied and ran off to the sanctuary of my bedroom.

Tuesday, 30th October:
Vung Tau is popular for its proximity to Ho Chi Minh, that's all: in other words, it's scarcely what you'd imagine a beach resort to be, whether in South–East Asia or elsewhere. We did discover an attractive strip of sand, but the water looked too polluted to risk. We also found two huge Buddhas — one reclining at a temple named Niet Ban Tinh Xa, and a fascinating site called Thich Ca Phat Dai with cheap souvenir and drink stalls. Prices were just ridiculously low and to be fair I bought something at each kiosk. At one of the temples, we met two charming girls, who showed us around and gave us free drinks. They went all coy when I suggested taking their photo: the kindness and spontaneity of the Vietnamese have been the best memory of the trip for sure.

Wednesday, 31st October:
We wend our way back to Ho Chi Minh . . . to the tune of the 'Lambada'.
Return to the Lao Consulate. The policeman at the gate takes one look at Iew and remarks: *"Kampuchea? Where passport?"* Horrified, Iew hands over his red document and firmly asserts *"Thai."* *"You?"* he inquires of me. *"Me English."* We are allowed in. The building seems empty. Eventually a man appears, grumpy and dishevelled, as if woken reluctantly from his siesta. It is my first encounter with a Laotian.

"Visa for Laos?" I inquire with no optimism.

"Not possible," comes the expected reply. Then silence.

"How much visa for Laos: And how long take?" I continue in my clearest broken English. The words 'how much' have caused a stirring somewhere deep within.

"Visa take long time. Maybe two week, maybe three."

"But I leave Ho Chi Minh tomorrow. I must have tomorrow."

He sighs and shakes his head. *"Sorry, cannot."*
I sense a hesitation in his speech. I feel he is waiting for some kind of offer. I had deliberately not brought a gift with me to avoid temptation.

At times like this, when the hidden meaning is obvious to both parties, conversation takes on a weird, almost surreal style. I repeat my intentions: *"I leave tomorrow. Visa possible?"* I sense he is yielding: *"Possible, but expensive."* And that was as far as we got. He explained that the visa was only valid for entry into Laos from Ho Chi Minh City and not from Bangkok. So not only would I have had to re–route completely, but worse still, chance either Hang Khong or Lao Aviation. Nonetheless, it had been a fascinating battle of innuendoes.

Thursday, 1st November:
Little to do today except to hang about and wait for the flight. At fifty-five dollars, my call home is the most expensive I've ever made.

We are about to leave for the airport when our guide comes rushing up to us with the news that the flight has been delayed. He doesn't know how late it'll be (though Air France's office is adjacent to the Doc Lap Hotel). So it looks like a long wait at Tan Son Nhat Airport.

The driver's English hasn't improved, nor has his cassette collection. Thank God it's only a short journey.

The queue at the check–in counter is surprisingly short: I wonder where all the passengers have gone to. But there they are, attempting to get through customs. It's a complete disarray: the French fussing and grumbling as usual, the Thais shaking their heads and muttering more than just 'mai ben lai', and only the Vietnamese at one with the performance. I just watch the mayhem: have I filled out the right forms? Have I sold anything? Did I declare everything on my arrival? And what about the money I changed on the black market? With five hours still to wait, what's the hurry? Let's have a few more Saigon Exports — what, they've run out? No problem. Warm Pepsi will do.

Eventually I go through. My luggage is thoroughly searched, and the official waves me on. It's only then that I remember the X–ray machine isn't film–safe and that most of my shots of Vietnam are now just a blur . . .

Friday, 2nd November:
We have a few days to wait in Bangkok before flying up to Chiang Mai: as fate would have it, my camera is stolen from my hotel room. The unlucky 'kamoy' will not only have acquired a camera which cost me just a 'pony' from Dixons in Bayswater, but also a number of indistinguisable scenes of Vietnam.

Tuesday, 6th November:
Chiang Mai is once again seething with tourists and, with no 'Lin geh how' to call upon, I 'tuk–tuk' frantically about town in a vain search for cheap accommodation. No other choice but to lodge at the Chiang Inn, in the core of the Night Bazaar, a two thousand baht a night heart–breaker.

It isn't long before curiosity gets the better of me, and I am once again sneaking timidly down Charoenprathet Soi 6. The sign 'Rin's Rooms for Rent' still hangs, alliterative and beckoning, but no Rin, and no 'Rooms for Rent'. Just 'Gem Travel'. And a smart alick from Northern Ireland.

Gleefully, he relates the woeful tale of the fall of the 'geh how': of how John and Rin sold out to Nancy and her rich Japanese husband Wattanabe. I remember Nancy, a friend of Rin's (if such a person existed): she took advantage of Iew's collapsed jewellery business by buying up all his stock. Retribution has come full circle. Now I'll never find out if she intended to call it 'Guest House of Nancy's'.

Gem Travel is yet another in the seemingly endless list of trekking compa-nies to spring up in Chiang Mai in recent years. The smug proprietor, with his subservient Thai wife, makes no secret of the fact that his only ambition is to take the tourist for as many baht as possible. A successful tour company in Chiang Mai need offer the 'farang' very little (save for the odd westernized and exploited hilltribe), but in return can make a veritable mint. Aside from talking about himself and denigrating everyone else in Chiang Mai, he tells me that John and Rin are still living together in Lamphun. He is about to direct a tirade of abuse at the eccentric duo, when I take my leave. For me, 'Rin's Rooms for Rent' were sacred and their memory should be respected.

It is with a heavy heart that I walk off down the 'soi'. Once so vibrant, so unpredictable, 'Lin's Looms for Lent' (as Iew would say) are no more. No more scenes or dramas, no more tantrums, no more customers, no more 'nam prik ong'. As I approach the Night Bazaar, I am brutally woken from my nostalgic reverie: a 'tuk–tuk' comes hurtling round the corner and narrowly avoids despatching me into premature nirvana.

Chiang Mai's Nigel Mansell?

Wednesday, 7th November:
Yang trees line the route from Chiang Mai to Lamphun, evoking memories of the Parisian boulevards. It's a scenic journey that takes about twenty minutes in bus or 'songthaew'. This is my second trip but I cannot recall Rin's house. Fortunately Iew remembers and he taps violently on the roof of the 'songthaew' with his five baht piece to inform the driver. With no respect for his brakes or the other passengers, he brings the pick–up to a sudden screeching halt.

I would certainly have had trouble finding the house, armed solely with the address in English, for '271 Pa Hew Soi 2 Moo 7 T. Umong A. Muang

Lamphun 51150' probably wouldn't have got me very far. It reads more like a garbled order from a Chinese takeaway than an address in Thailand. A foul smell pervades the house. This becomes more acrid as I walk towards the lavatory: it's not that Rin has flushed a husband down the loo — impossible because they haven't got a flush, only a bucket. No: all soon becomes clear. Rin's mother has a mini fishmonger's at the rear. She is busy preparing the 'catch'. We 'wai' respectfully and proffer a *'sawatdee kup'*.

It always intrigues me the different manner in which 'farangs' and Thais greet old friends who drop by unexpectedly. Whereas we will show delight, surprise and even astonishment and say things like *"My God, I can't believe it"* or *"fancy bumping into you again"* or *"what a surprise. How wonderful to see you,"* the Thais express little emotion. I have noticed this on many occasions, even with families. I know of a Thai who hadn't seen his grandmother for almost twenty years, turning up out of the blue on her doorstep. Her response — a simple *"bai nai?"* which they say means *"where you go?"* I doubt my grandmother's reaction would be so unconcerned and reserved. More like *"Why the f**k haven't you been to see me for twenty years you ungrateful bastard"* . . . or, seeing that she lives in the suburbs of Paris, whatever the French equivalent would be. Perhaps the Thais are just more honest and less hypocritical. Or, more probably, less bothered.

So John and I were reminiscing over a glass of Lamphun's best bottled water and a bowl of glass noodles, while Iew and Rin, quite unconcerned, were gossiping and giggling. They were more interested in the five baht comics which Iew had bought earlier that day.

The second edition of *A Trekkers Guide to the Hill Tribes of Northern Thailand* is out, and John has kindly given me an acknowledgement. His *Hilltribe Phrase Book* is on its way, to be followed by a third tome, *Touring Northern Thailand.* How quickly old grievances — and twenty-seven thousand baht — are forgotten. Always rather uncertain, disorganised and eccentric — but essentially 'jai dee' as the Thais say — John seems to have gone downhill since our last encounter in June. He relates all kinds of tales: of woe, disaster, confusion. Of separation and reunion, of suicide threats and bodged attempts (on her behalf, naturally), of bizarre happenings. But they're still together: and as they say in France 'Plus ça change, plus c'est la même chose' (the more things change, the more they stay the same).

We celebrate our reconciliation that evening at a new restaurant in Chiang Mai called 'Once Upon A Time', where most of the waiters are 'kateuys'. It is situated in a marvellously scenic location, by the Ping River — try not to sit too close to the water or the mosquitoes will have *you* for dinner — and built in traditional Northern Thai style. The food, alas, is quite ordinary.

Northern Thai food is quite distinct from that served elsewhere. Forget about the tourist–pushed 'Khantoke' dinners — yet another example (if one's needed) of a gimmick to con the hapless 'farang' — and go instead for the much–maligned 'kao niaow' ('sticky' rice), 'larb gai' or 'larb moo' (a spicy salad of minced chicken or pork with chillies and mint) and the delicious 'nam prik ong' — a sort of spicy minced pork dip.

Thursday, 8th November:
We have four days before our trip to Burma and I'm a bit restless hanging about in Chiang Mai. I had hoped to get to Mae Hong Son — which borders Burma to the north west — but it's so popular with 'farangs' (Mae Hong Son is being thoroughly hyped by the trekking companies as an alternative to Chiangs Mai and Rai) that all the seats on the plane are taken. It's a short hop from Chiang Mai by plane — yet a gruelling nine hours by bus. So I'll have to look elsewhere. I take out my Thai Airways domestic timetable, and see where they fly to on Fridays. Phitsanulok. Where my first English students back in March hailed from. I'd never heard of it then, but I shall see it tomorrow.

Friday, 9th November:
Prior to my two–day stint in Phitsanulok, I drop by the Tax Clearance Office to check if I'm OK to leave for Burma on Monday. The 'tuk–tuk' driver takes me to the wrong building and refuses to budge until I pay. I'm not in the mood for an argument. This looks like being one helluva day. I can just sense it.

The old sourpuss is still taking her bribes in the Tax Office. I wait my turn. Before me is a clever dick from the States who speaks fluent Thai. Somehow that always irks me — must be jealousy. The bint beckons me to sit down. I smile and explain my position.

"Passport," she demands without a trace of the fabled national charm.

She shudders, shakes her head and utters one word: *"Bangkok."*
"Bangkok?" I reply. *"Cannot. Today I go Phitsanulok and Monday Burma."* I bet my broken English is better than the Yank's.

"Before you go Burma, you go Tack Office Bangkok." I explained that I was flying from Chiang Mai, and *not* from Bangkok. Then she muttered something about financial guarantees from various people. I couldn't follow what she was saying. There was an increasing number of impatient 'farangs' waiting their turn, and I could perceive she was losing her patience. She got out her calculator, worked out how many days I had spent in Thailand, and shook her head again. *"Cannot leave Thailand,"* she concluded.

"I must. I go Monday." What a shame I didn't have a bottle of whisky handy.

"Cannot. You go Bangkok before." She'd had enough. She gestured me to leave with a flick of the hand, and turned her attention to the next in the

queue. She smiled unctuously at him, in the knowledge that she had safely humiliated me.

It is a fifty minute flight from Chiang Mai to Phitsanulok — in an ageing and bumpy Shorts 360 — and for some reason the plane is full of French tourists. At the airport, hopeful hotel staff stand around with signs advertising the name of their accommodation, and touts sidle up to you whispering *"taxi, taxi"*. *Never* look as though you don't know where you're going and *never* consult a map in public. For, as if by magic, someone will mysteriously appear and . . . if not rip you off, then lead you astray. You see you are never without company in the 'Land of (the teeth behind the) Smiles'.

Phitsanulok was badly damaged by a fire in 1959: I don't know what it looked like then, but today it's a dump, vying with Nan for the title of 'ugliest city in Thailand'. It has a row of concrete shoeboxes masquerading as shops. The Amarin Nakorn Hotel (recommended by the guide–books) is overpriced and characterless, but serves fascinating fare — 'Pork Shop' and 'Prawns Throb' to name but two of the many alluring dishes. And a notice in my room announces that the hotel forbids 'prostitutes and called girls'. The sole redeeming feature of Phitsanulok is the splendid Jinaraj Buddha inside Wat Mahathat.

Saturday, 10th November:
'Farangs' are something of a rarity here, and the curious locals stare intently as I walk by. Shop assistants beckon me inside to look at goods I have no intention of buying. Two girls, who work in an optician's shop, attract my attention. Timid at first, they are determined to entice me in and sell me a pair of 'Ray Ban' sunglasses. Now sunglasses are no good to me, since I need my own prescription lenses, but they persist. They give me a drink, offer me a seat and then titter. They ask me to make a price for the glasses. *"Mai ao,"* I reply. They don't give up, for so few 'farangs' pass their way. I yield. I make what I deem to be a derisory offer: the girl disappears to consult the manageress, then returns. *"OK, no probrem. One thousand two hundred baht."* She agrees. I borrow her calculator — twenty-five pounds for a pair of genuine 'Ray Bans'. A bargain. Only on leaving does it occur to me that I don't want — and can't use — the glasses and that they couldn't possibly be genuine in any case. But I feel uplifted by the kindness and hospitality of the people.

Sunday, 11th November:
I have no tickets, and very little information about tomorrow's trip to Burma, and yet I cannot recall the last time I was on such a high. I have immersed myself in all kinds of books about the country and its politics. It seems to grip me more and more as the day nears. I hope I will not be disappointed.

Monday, 12th November:
The minibus that is supposed to pick us up at six am never shows and with time running out we flag down a 'tuk–tuk'. I have no idea what's going on: at the airport there is no information. I can only wait. But I espy a Bangkok Airways twin–prop on the tarmac.

I approach a 'farang': his name is Michel and he is French. *"So you are Monsieur Greenwood. We wait for you since long time. We must go to the VIP room. You have your passport?"* I hand it over. He takes one peep inside and a look of horror passes over him. *"You are journalist?"* I remember how proud I felt the day I went to the Passport Office in Petty France to have my occupation changed from 'Student' to 'Racing journalist'. Now it appears I was living to regret it.

"You know the position regarding journalists in Burma?" he asked rather unnecessarily.

I feigned ignorance. *"No. Is there a problem?"*

"Problème? This is terrible." He walked off and showed my passport to the other organisers of the group. For many months they had been negotiating with the notoriously intransigent Burmese authorities to set up these tours, of which we were only the second. Geneviève Goux, the French lady ostensibly responsible for the arrangements, summoned me over. She was flustered and at a loss for words. It was fortunate I spoke French. Journalists, she explained, were forbidden to enter Burma and if she had known I was a journalist (in whatever field) I would never have been allowed to book. It was not my fault, but that of the travel agent. However, seeing as I was here (and had paid), there was nothing to be done. She advised me, that since Burma was going through a particularly sensitive period, I was to keep my head low and not to talk to any Burmese. In all probability, she concluded, I would be sent back to Thailand on the first available flight. Crumbs, I thought, not on Burma Airways . . .

Our group consisted essentially of photographers and tour operators. The photographers — two very British girls working in Singapore — were there to obtain publicity shots for travel brochures. But there were Thais, a German girl, and an elderly French couple. Most were staying just one day in Pagan before flying on to Mandalay and back to Chiang Mai. Only the French couple (known solely as 'Madame et Monsieur'), Iew (whose French consisted of *'Bonjour, ça va, comment allez–vous? Ça va bien, merci et vous?'*) and I were actually part of the tour.

Sitting in the VIP lounge, I have to fill out a myriad of entry forms — and, no doubt if I'm going to be deported on arrival, departure forms too. Iew struggles to write English, so that doubles the task. We have no tickets, no boarding passes and no one has checked the luggage. We are ready to embark. There are no stewardesses — smiling or otherwise — or safety instructions, no interminably dull in–flight magazines and, more drastically, no sick–bags. I thought we might be aboard another Dash 8, but the pilot mumbles something about an EMB–120 (you can never understand announcements, particularly in Thai), which apparently is a Brazilian design. That fills me with enormous confidence. As the propellers begin to rotate, the noise is deafening. I don't dare look out, instead sit there wondering whether we're going at all fast enough to make it, there is a 'whoosh' and we are airborne. Ninety minutes of sheer terror.

I worry about everything. A night in Pagan jail, deportation. And then I suddenly remember: they never mentioned my Tax Clearance Certificate. I had escaped, after all. The adventure was just beginning.

Having barely got to grips with Thai characters — by which I mean vowels and consonants — Burmese letters appear extraordinary. All circles, C's and bubbles. I practise the sounds from my phrase–book as we fly over the Shan Hills.

"For 'mingala' say 'Mengele': mingala baa, mingala baa, mingala baa . . ."

By now I have become a little braver and I glance outside. The views are spectacular. For some reason — Burmese bureaucracy, I suspect — we are not permitted to fly directly to Pagan: we must go over Mandalay. From high I can spot the glinting pagodas, and a river which I presume to be the Irrawaddy. Touchdown is perfect.

Burma's not-so-secret police.

Pagan Airport is actually located at Nyaung U, some ten kilometres from the town. We are met by several official–looking types. I notice Geneviève (who speaks the language) immediately strike up conversation with a Burmese. Since she glances at me from time to time, I assume she is talking about my 'profession'. She edges closer to me as surreptitiously as possible: *"I have spoken to the official,"* she says. *"I think it'll be OK as long as you keep your head down* (she keeps saying that). *You'll be followed by the secret police until they realize that you're all right. So don't talk to anyone for the moment."* For whatever reason, the secret police make no attempt to conceal their identity. Bar the guides, they are the only Burmese with us constantly: and, not only do they follow my every move, but they also stare at me continually — and not very subtly.

Burmese bureaucracy is notorious — even amongst Asian travellers who have had an awful lot to put up with — and since we were only the second ever international flight to land at Nyaung U, Immigration and Customs were guaranteed to be a major performance. A vast entourage, much conferring with superiors, much needless doodling on paper. But we were through in an hour: a tremendous achievement for Burmese officialdom.

It was only when the Customs officer was rummaging through my rucksack that I remembered that I had a copy of Bertil Lintner's latest book on the imprisoned Burmese leader Aung San Suu Kyi. Not surprisingly Swedish journalist Lintner — whose previous book *Outrage* describes in graphic detail the student uprisings of 1988 — is 'persona non grata' in Burma and his books are banned. I shudder to think what sort of effect the tome would have on the Customs man. I would most certainly be on the next flight home — Burma Air or not. But he seemed more concerned with finding items which I might sell on — like cameras or Walkmans (Walkmen?) — and fortunately didn't discover the book.

Our guide is everything I'd expected a Burmese lady to be — elegant, gentle, cultured and refined. She has a vast knowledge of Pagan and remarkably — or so it seems to me — can remember the names of all the temples and pagodas. That is something I'd never manage to do.

We are taken off in the 'state–run' bus of Myanmar Travel and Tours. A creaky old yellow contraption with no air conditioning, it has obviously seen better days. The poor guide has trouble making herself heard above the racket of the engine. Now this poses an additional problem for the French couple Madame and Monsieur — since not only can they understand little English, they also can't hear a word the guide is saying. I have offered to act as interpreter to them, but already after a few minutes I am rueing my magnanimity. My knowledge, alas, of the French terminology for temples and pagodas is sadly lacking and I am being pestered repeatedly with *"Qu'est–ce que'elle a dit?"*, *"Quoi?"* and *"Comment?"*. I am losing my patience. They have already moaned several times about there being a non French–speaking guide. *"But they promise somebody who speak French"* grumbles Monsieur.

But even they can't deflect my attention from this vast tide of pagodas. Words alone cannot hope to describe the breathtaking beauty, the aura, the magnificence that is Pagan. It is quite unlike anything I have witnessed before. So many times the camera shutters click, so many times the bus grinds to a sudden halt and we hasten outside to catch another fleeting glimpse of a golden pagoda.

The route from Nyaung U takes in the wonderful Shwezigon Pagoda. With its golden stupa, the Shwezigon is one of the most sacred pagodas in the land. It is said to contain relics of the Buddha. It is far more splendid than anything I have ever seen in Thailand.

We are invited to lunch at the house of a well–to–do Burmese family, friends of the guide. It is a great honour and we are treated with deference and respect that is so much a part of Burmese — and indeed South–East Asian — society. The meal consists of a soup (as is invariably the case in Burma), noodles and a chicken curry. It lacks the colour, distinctiveness and quality that stamp Thai cuisine, rather it is bland and insipid. But the hospitality cannot be faulted. This is obviously a special occasion for the family: the children have taken the day off school and are dressed in their finest traditional costumes. To conclude the meal, we are each handed an orange and a cheroot.

Back in the bus, Madame and Monsieur are still moaning. It's too hot, too uncomfortable . . . the list of complaints never ends. They are going to be trouble, for sure. Tomorrow it will be just them and us, for the remainder of the group is flying on to Mandalay. Oh, I forgot . . . and the not–so–secret police.

We are accommodated at the Thiripyitsaya Hotel, which has the reputation of being Burma's finest. At first glance it certainly looks impressive, set out, as it is, in magnificent grounds overlooking the Irrawaddy River. The rooms are individual bungalows spread out over quite a wide area (supposedly with air conditioning, though I haven't yet been able to get mine to work). There is a swimming pool, a verandah (popular with the more affluent members of Pagan society), a restaurant and a puppet theatre, a traditional Pagan treat. Like so much of South–East Asia, the hotel looks good from the outside . . . but scratch the surface and what do you find? The swimming pool is out of order, along with my air conditioning, the restaurant serves lukewarm, bland Sino–Burmese cuisine and worst of all, rumour has it that they run out of Mandalay beer with regular monotony. The 'bathroom' could only be Burmese — the shower has a life of its own and the water switches quite unpredictably from hot to cold.

We end the afternoon by paying a visit to a local village. The reaction of the children to us is just like that of a Northern Thai hilltribe. Curious and inquisitive, they refuse to leave our side. Their faces do not tire of smiling. Walking through the village, I narrowly avoid being felled by a herd of stampeding cows. This amuses the villagers greatly and they collapse into rumbustious laughter.

Even Burmese cattle flee from Ne Win.

We catch the sunset high up a pagoda: a magnificent sight over the spell-binding plains of Pagan. It has been a truly unforgettable day and I collapse, exhausted, into bed quite unconcerned about the antics of the whimsical Burmese air conditioning.

Tuesday, 13th November:
The majority of the group has gone on to Mandalay and just the four of us are left — Madame, Monsieur, Iew and I. The hotel staff seems to take little interest in the guests: those who work in the restaurant are particularly surly.

It is another day spent helter–skelter, from temple to temple, pagoda to pagoda. We stop only briefly to take refreshment and then, finally, call in at the house of a 'friend'. He is a dealer of some description, gems, currency, lacquerware — and anything else that is currently available in Burma. Now was the time to fulfil a long–held ambition: to purchase a 'genuine' Burmese ruby. He showed me his collection, convincingly wrapped up in a fifteen kyat note. I selected a pink stone, which he assured me was a fine example of a Burmese ruby. But was I falling for the same routine which I had so strongly castigated back in Thailand? Maybe, but I think I wanted to be duped.

Burmese bargaining: I greeted his gambit of fifty US dollars with feigned astonishment and countered with one of fifteen. He looked equally aghast, but dropped the price to forty. I advanced mine slightly to twenty — I had set myself a maximum of twenty-five. There is an art to haggling in South–East Asia: always look horrified at the opening offer which must be immediately halved, keep the bargaining good–natured and never deride the vendor. Neither the seller nor the prospective purchaser must lose face — if a deal *is* struck, both parties must feel — or at least give the impression — that they have done well out of the sale. Never lose your temper, but be prepared to walk away if you are not satisfied with the 'final' offer. Chances are the vendor will call you back and accept your price.

"Thirty dollars. My last price," said the Burmese.

"Sorry, I cannot give more than twenty. I have little money. The official rate is very bad at the hotel," I replied.

"I help you. You want to change money? I give you rate twelve times better than official rate." And so he did.

One of the most maddening features of Burma under Ne Win was the outrageous currency exchange swindle: tourists were obliged to change a certain amount of money — of course, it should have been all — at a derisory rate (roughly six kyat to the dollar), yet sixty kyat were freely available on the black market.

"I cannot sell for twenty dollars — I make no profit," he pleaded. *"I make no profit"* is heard all too often. What is actually meant is *"These goods have been marked up at least five hundred per cent but I want to squeeze even more out of you."* Still it's a good way of getting sympathy — and with that, the upper hand.

"OK, twenty–one dollars," I concede.

"Twenty–five."

"Twenty–two."

"Twenty–three." I wasn't going to budge from that figure. He tried to extract another dollar out of me but I wouldn't yield. So we shook hands on twenty–three, both delighted to have concluded a satisfactory deal. And, more importantly, no one had lost face.

Our transaction over, he offered me tea and we talked. He wasn't nearly as reticent as I suspected he would be. Things were bad, sure, but they'd been bad before. The Burmese were used to waiting: they were good Buddhists and some day things would have to change. But he kept intimating that they couldn't change while 'He' (Ne Win) was still alive. So they'd wait, and wait: and we in the West would never fully understand. Life went on, business was OK and nobody starved.

1. Wat Po, Bangkok: This magnificent temple is home to the vast Reclining Buddha, not to mention a school of Thai 'traditional massage'.

2. *Chiang Mai: One of the city's many colourful festivals. A bevy of Thai beauties display their wares.*

3. Northern Thailand: Deforested but stunning nonetheless. View over-looking Chiang Saen and the Mekhong River.

4. Chiang Saen, Northern Thailand: The Mekhong River is one of the most majestic in all Asia, and forms the border between Thailand and Laos.

5. *Mae Sai, Northern Thailand: The Thai/Burma Border. Counterfeit gems and fake hilltribe girls: perfected tourist rip-off.*

6. Typical Thai 'sanuk': A pop concert held in a Northern Thai temple.

7. *Nan province, Northern Thailand: 'Phi Tong Luang', Spirits of the Yellow Leaves.*

8. Only around a hundred 'Phi Tong Luang' still remain. Lucky for the faithful hound his master isn't an Akha. Barbecued dogs are their speciality.

9. *Black Lahu man clad in his New Year's costume: All set for a rendition of 'Auld Lang Syne'?*

10. Lisu girl also in New Year's garb: Ready to see in 1993 with a bang.

11. Karen woman bearing a food basket: Rubies fresh in from Burma?

12. General store, Doi Mae Salong, Northern Thailand: A predominantly Chinese town of Kuomintang, refugees from the communist revolution of 1949.

13. Hilltribe children desperate to catch a glimpse of next seasons's Derby winner. What's Akha for 'Go on Lester'?

14. Ho Chi Minh City, Vietnam: Still known affectionately as Saigon. Struggling into the 1990s, vibrant, alluring, poverty–stricken.

15. Vietnam: A typical scene. This one will never make it to Epsom!

16, 17 and 18 (following pages). Pagan, Burma: If there are more stunning views than these in all of South–East Asia, I'll just have to keep on travelling.

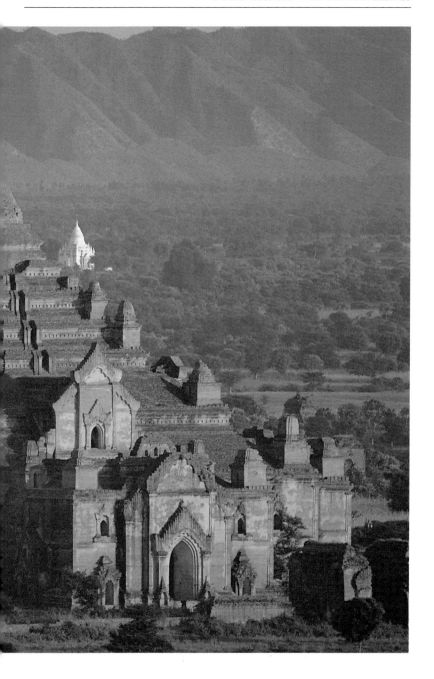

19. Mandalay, Burma: Feeble and ineffective attempts at propaganda by the evil, dim-witted Burmese military.

20. Mingun, Burma: My guide Iew. Even a Thai couldn't fail to be moved by the splendour of this beautiful land.

21. *Novice monks in Mandalay: The setting for some of the most brutal repression carried out by the Burmese military, including the shooting of monks.*

22. North East Thailand: 'Fares please'. A nightmare job being a conductor of this 'Isaan' mode of transport.

23. Khon Kaen, North East Thailand: Two 'samlor' drivers take a well earned break after a heavy meal perhaps of 'sticky' rice and 'somtam' (papaya salad).

24. North East Thailand: An apprentice rider limbering up in anticipation of the 1993 'Isaan' Grand National.

25. *Wat Kaek, Nong Khai: A sight even more frightening than that of the meat-cleaver wielding Rin. A Hindu–Buddhist temple in 'Isaan'.*

26. Luang Prabang, Northern Laos: Stunning view of sunset over the Mekhong River.

27. Luang Prabang: Hilltribe villagers and Laotians mingle in the early morning mist by the Mekhong River.

28. *Luang Prabang: A Laotian novice monk. A frequent sight wherever you wander in this wonderful town.*

29. Luang Prabang: Two Laotian children pose in front of what appears to be a rather strange flower-pot, left over from the Vietnam War, perhaps.

30. Bangkok: The ubiquitous 'tuk–tuk'. When not weaving its way through the terrible traffic, the 'tuk–tuk' ('samlor') has its other uses!

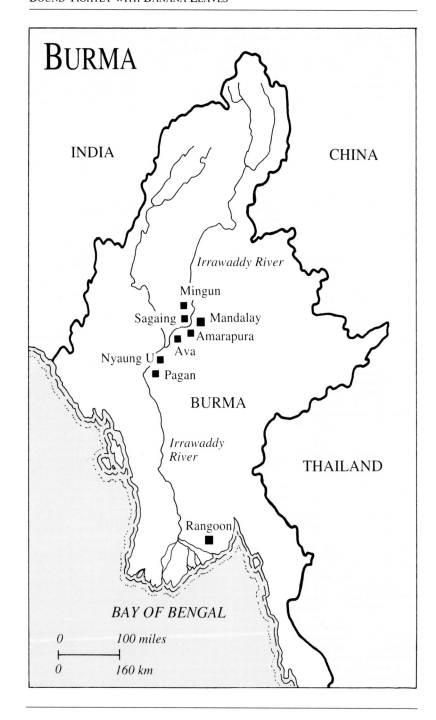

I wasn't sure how to respond to this extraordinarily relaxed — if not resigned — attitude, so typically Buddhist, so typically Burmese. For it's anathema to us in the West, where we are brought up on a philosophy of push, push, push, and where achievement and advancement count for everything. We aren't bred to sit around waiting for change, waiting for something to happen. 'Godot' never comes — the very opposite of the Thai (and Buddhist) concept of 'mai ben lai'. One felt that Ne Win should stand up and proclaim to all, those immortal words of Harold Macmillan (the text somewhat altered, of course), *"You've never had it so bad"*. But maybe for once it wasn't for us in the West to impose our own will on things. Change would come in its own time — and that was certainly the way the Burmese dealer looked upon it.

We are interrupted by the impatient grumblings of Monsieur and Madame. But if they don't keep me sweet, I might mistranslate. Both in their seventies, he is barely capable of getting into and out of the minibus. Each time we stop — and on a two–day whirlwind tour of Pagan that's pretty frequently — he has to be assisted by either the guide or Iew. You could not possibly imagine someone more ill–equipped to partake in such a journey, and with Madame fussing about him with typical Gallic histrionics, the whole scenario is irritating to say the least. However, you had to admire their determination and guts — they'd travelled all over the globe, and weren't going to be deterred by a rickety old bus or a steep climb up a pagoda.

No one hurries in Burma; there's no need and it's just too oppressive. Round every corner there's another temple and in each temple, souvenir sellers, touts, students wanting to practise their English (since the uprising of 1988 the universities had remained shut), and the simply curious. All have something to sell, to exchange — or just a tale to tell. Instead of the Thai *"Where you come from mister?"* you're greeted with a courteous *"And what is your country, sir?"*

"You swop T–shirt? You have cigarettes? Whisky? Lipstick?. Perfume?" — well I can't say I carry the last two items around with me regularly. Or, of course, the ubiquitous *"change money?"* Iew is bemused at the repeated requests to swop T–shirts: he's never seen anything like this in Thailand and is busy rummaging through his suitcase for items to exchange. He's very taken with the Burmese (praise indeed coming from a Thai), and, curiously enough, were he clad in 'longyi' himself could well be mistaken for a Shan.

Time, alas, draws on and the pagodas go by. The Ananda Temple is perhaps the best known in Pagan, but others are equally memorable. At one, however, we are refused entry much to the disappointment of the guide. The rumour is that "Number One's" sidekick, leader of SLORC (State Law and Order Restoration Council) Saw Maung is visiting Pagan. There is a noticeable army presence around many of the temples. They smile at us: it's hard to believe that just over two years ago they were massacring students in Rangoon and monks in Mandalay.

From Saw Maung to Pagan's puppets, marvellous creations which, alas, make for a rather tedious show. Sipping my nightcap on the verandah of the Thiripyitsaya Hotel, I strike up conversation with a local farmer who insists on talking in a whisper and continually glances over his shoulder. It seems an ordeal, a risk for him to be seen talking to a foreigner: the secret police, he believes, may be watching him. I can't really hear most of what he says, but I get the gist. It turns out to be an almost Thai-like sob–story, though I have more sympathy with him than with his Siamese neighbours. But the tale concludes the same way — in a plea for money. Burmese kyat — for if he's caught with dollars (or trying to exchange them) he'll be in trouble. I explain I only have dollars — ah well, no problem, he can take dollars after all. I give him a five dollar bill. I never found out his name. He only told me that my ruby was certainly a fake.

Consume several bottles of Mandalay beer whilst watching the Irrawaddy flow past. Could there be a more magnificent setting? I doubt it; shame about the mosquitoes, though.

Wednesday, 14th November:
We're on the road to Mandalay; at least we're off to Pagan Airport to catch the Bangkok Airways flight to Mandalay. Since this is Burma, the flight is late. I ask how late, but no one seems to know. Do they have any information at all? Now in Burma, you see, just no one says 'No': it's taboo to upset anyone — particularly a foreigner — or to lose face (yes, that Asian concept again) by not having an answer. So, in response to the question: *"Do you have any information on the flight from Chiang Mai?"*, the reply would be something akin to: *"It wouldn't help you to make that sort of inquiry."* Or something equally gobbledegook. And when I suggest they telephone Chiang Mai Airport for information, they just smile. I wonder how the outsiders who work in this strange land cope with this kind of mentality?

Our luggage is thoroughly searched, but I have already passed on the book of Aung San Suu Kyi to a Burmese friend. We while away the time in a food–stall opposite the entrance to the airport. I say 'food–stall', but that's a misnomer. They sold a type of peanut candy, a few beers and a lemon pop. Well it was supposed to be lemon pop only the label had come off. How many times had that particular bottle been re–used? Six, seven, ten?

After a couple of hours I hear a whirring in the Pagan skies. The EMB–120 is approaching. I pay my bill but notice that my customs declaration form is missing — *"no problem"* says the guide in true Burmese fashion. I'm not convinced the Mandalay authorities will be so lax.

Mandalay is just a half–hour flight from Pagan, with a spectacular approach over the hills. The twin–prop then drops rapidly as it nears the airstrip: for one awful moment I feel as though we are plummeting into the Mandalay turf. Just like Kipling's flying fish.

Ah Mandalay, Mandalay — what images are evoked by your very name. But not the images I'd anticipated: I am greeted instead by large red signs proclaiming:
"Crush all destructive elements"
"The Tatmadaw will never betray the National cause"
"Only when there is discipline, will there be progress"
And no one takes any notice.

Mandalay had been a hotbed of political activity for years and was the setting for some of the most heinous crimes committed by the military during the junta's crackdown, including, of course, the murder of several monks. There is a strong army presence in the town now and a curfew every evening at eleven o'clock.

Mandalay is a vast town: hot and dusty. It seems to spread itself over a large terrain. There are only two hotels open to tourists — the Mya Mandala and the — surprise, surprise — Mandalay. A large, colonial–style establishment, dirty, run–down and characterless, it makes Pagan's Thiripyitsaya Hotel look like the Oriental. My room is squalid, the air–conditioner doesn't work and the bathroom resembles something out of the hilltribes. The shower is erratic and only spurts out cold water: still, Mandalay's so stuffy, warm water, I suppose, is an unnecessary luxury. I'm at least grateful that Madame and Monsieur next door do have hot water, but there's still plenty for them to moan about. Not least the food in the restaurant . . . and let's not forget the Mandalay Hotel bar, described in one guide–book as "positively grim". I, for one, wouldn't dispute that.

Breakfast and supper were dished up in different corners of the hotel: but that didn't make a scrap of difference to either the service or, alas, to the cuisine. Invariably it arrived lukewarm and — not to put too fine a point on it — tasteless. Whether they were worried about foreigners finding Burmese fare too spicy, who can say. But they toned down the heat to such an extent that the result was a sort of poor man's bland Chinese cooking. Each meal started with a soup that was always completely insipid and con-cluded with an orange which contained an extraordinary number of pips. The waiters, too, were offish — a long way removed from the charming Burmese we had hitherto met. Needless to say, those purveyors of *haute cuisine* — Monsieur and Madame — were not best pleased. But in the end, they just shrugged their shoulders and tucked in along with the rest of us.

Mandalay is a sprawling city, in some ways like Bangkok — and one in which only the mad walk. Most of the population take to their bikes or cling on for dear life to some form of pick–up truck (not unlike the Thai 'songthaews'). Thus there is no organised traffic flow or right of way. Bikes compete with horse carts and two–seated cyclos — one facing the front and one the back — along with other typically Asian contraptions. There is simply no order, but plenty of tooting of horns. Delightful chaos.

We stop off first at Zegyo Market. Situated in the town centre and over-looked by the Diamond Jubilee Clock (dating from Queen Victoria's reign), Zegyo Market is, quite simply, vast. It was designed in 1903 by an Italian called Count Caldrari, first secretary of the Mandalay municipality. Everything — and I mean everything — is on sale: all kinds of fruit and vegetables (shame the hotel chef didn't do his shopping there), goods of various descriptions (many, to Iew's joy, smuggled in from Thailand), che-roots, toys, clothes, weird fish I'd never set eyes on before (and hopefully never would again), nuts, tobacco, all manner of things to chew on . . . and a real Burmese favourite — grasshoppers. Well they *may* have been locusts, or even crickets. But whatever they were, they gave me the creeps. But the locals — and alas Iew too — loved them: stir–fried with oil in a wok. I didn't pry further into what other kinds of creepy–crawlies were frying that night, though later I discovered some kids in the road outside the hotel catching cockroaches, tying them up in their T–shirts (which they were still wearing) and taking them home for supper. And I grumbled about the food at the hotel . . .

There is little to keep the youth of Mandalay occupied. With the universities yet to re–open, the students hang out at the tea–shops (I met a few at the quaintly and very colonially named 'Royal Orchid Tea' — they appeared to have omitted the word 'Shop' in the title) — and temples, desperate to strike up conversation with the foreign visitors. They are always deferential and extremely polite with an idiosyncratic command of the English language. Invariably they ask for your address, which they enter into their note–book — along with many others. They say they'll write — but they never do. They just seem fascinated with addresses, hoping to acquire as many as possible — and then very proud to show them off when you ask them. Of the innumerable crimes that the military junta have to answer for, this senseless waste of youth rates as one of the worst.

'Frying tonight' at Zegyo Market.

We took a Burmese–style 'songthaew' as far as we could up Mandalay Hill. As hard as you may have tried, you would not have been able to squeeze in another soul. We were clinging on desperately as we rounded each corner. The locals, of course, loved every minute of it. They were busy discussing the lottery, checking numbers to see if they'd won. Now I wasn't quite sure how it worked — according to our guide, the lottery — like so many other things — was banned by the military. So they wagered amongst themselves using the Thai lottery, which was quite legal, from over the border. The sooner they could obtain the results from the Thai press, the sooner they could fiddle the numbers and claim their rightful prize — at least that's how I think the system worked.

There are one thousand seven hundred and twenty-nine steps up Mandalay Hill, but fortunately we didn't have to climb them all. Nevertheless, the view — whilst not matching up to that of Pagan — was spectacular, taking in the Shan Hills and the Irrawaddy Plain. We rested at one of the drink stalls, surrounded by Burmese puffing at cheroots (the ladies, with their big cigars, looked quite extraordinary) and Iew attempted to chew betel. Betel is supposed to have an anaesthetic effect — as well as turning your teeth red (as any visitor to an Akha hilltribe village will have noticed). Iew, alas, finds it quite repulsive and spits it out — much to the amusement of the Burmese lady who sold it to him for a few kyat.

The only time we are left alone is when supper is over — by then, I presume, the authorities think we will be too tired to cause any mischief. But I am keen to explore further and Madame and Monsieur, too, despite their age, are enthusiastic. So, much to the hotel's chagrin, we take two cyclos and head off towards the night market. Now unlike the Thai and Vietnamese cyclos which hold two in the front, the Burmese variety seats one facing the fore and one the aft — if I'm not mixing my metaphors. This enables passengers to take evasive action against the unpredictable stream of vehicles which appear from all corners of the city.

With its curfew, Mandalay has no night life. Only a few shops stay open in the evening and the time is spent chatting over a few beers — if there are any available. How different the scene is over the border — just look at Chiang Mai's Night Bazaar. At eight pm, the night market here is winding down, though they soon wind up as they spot a rare tourist. Each stall–holder does his or her best to attract our attention, to beckon us over, to encourage us to part with our money. The range is limited: clothes, house-hold goods, grubby books, fruit and an array of Burmese desserts. The sweets are proffered freely and it would be impolite to refuse: we sample a few and smile but wander on. Frantically they call us back. I sense a sale to a foreigner is worth a large number of 'plus points'. And yet they seem more interested in acquiring goods off us: T–shirts, jewellery and most especially Iew's counterfeit Omega watch. Though at first reluctant to part with his timepiece, the persistency of their requests convinces him to offer it to the highest bidder. This happens to be an Indian gentleman (of which there are several with stalls) who tenders eleven hundred kyat. The Omega is now deified: it has become the object of worship and crowds flock round to gaze in admiration. Likewise the purchaser has achieved a new popular-ity. We are pestered for further items, but alas have none.

Now it so happens that one of the cyclo drivers has a sister who has a shop which sells . . . a familiar story? So, off we trundle across Mandalay to see the sister. Puffing on what must have been the largest cheroot in town, she welcomes us to her handicraft store. In excellent English, she explains that she can make special prices for us (?) and that she'll accept payment in kyat, baht or dollars. Did she have an old copy of the *FT* stashed away somewhere, for she knew the exchange rates exactly? And that was by no means the end: she could also change money at a most favourable rate and, best of all, show us her secret collection of precious stones. I often wondered where all the 'loobies from Burma' came from. Now I knew. Amazing how even the poorest farmer can lay his (or her) hands on a 'genuine' ruby.

The French pair was not impressed. They kept looking at their watches impatiently: they'd been through this old routine many times before. We took our leave: the shopkeeper's cheroot hadn't got much smaller. Maybe she'd still be smoking it when tomorrow came.

Monsieur meets his Waterloo in Mandalay.

Madame and Monsieur's cyclo arrived outside the hotel before ours (cyclos were not allowed inside the entrance) and Monsieur was just clambering out at his usual snail's pace, when we came hurtling round the corner. The driver couldn't stop in time and barged straight into poor Monsieur: he plopped to the ground like a ripe rambutan: 'zut alors'. Not that the driver understood the basics of French conversation, let alone the advanced stages of Gallic swearing. Monsieur was in no way badly hurt — merely shaken — but he gave a marvellous impression of 'The Dying Swan'. He hobbled off, shaking his fist and uttering all kind of obscenities. And naturally he refused to pay the driver. Monsieur was so mean that I wouldn't have been at all surprised if the entire performance had been stage–managed to avoid paying a few kyat.

I felt terribly sorry for the cyclo driver. He had taken us all round Mandalay for what to Monsieur, anyway, was a pittance. The Frenchman's antics were anathema to the Burmese: temper, criticism, raising the voice and finally loss of face. So I paid both drivers, told them not to worry and hurried back to the hotel to see how Monsieur was coping with his wounds. There was barely a graze on him. Wheresoever you journey, there will always be a discontented 'farang'. Even on the road to the Mandalay Hotel.

Thursday, 15th November:
I shan't bother any more with breakfasts at the hotel. They just defy description. In a land abounding in oranges, fresh orange juice is unavailable.

The Myanmar Travel and Tours bus carries us off to a local market (and a plethora of oranges), and we wend our way to the banks of the Irrawaddy. Not to watch the flying fish, alas, but the poor water buffaloes at work. The wretched creatures haul logs out of the river and up the slimy, muddy banks to the 'encouragement' of a whip–cracking, cheroot–puffing Burmese. The pitiful animals are exhausted by the time their task is completed. It doesn't do much to the soul.

From the market to the river we are followed by inquisitive, 'longyi'–clad kids. Winsome and cheeky, they never stop smiling and we go out of our way to buy them some biscuits at a local stall. Alas I have no gifts for them, save for some cleansing paper towels courtesy of Air France. Still, they are gratefully received — the children stare at them intently, confused and uncertain. I open one and pretend to wash my face. They stare, smile and giggle. Only then do they copy my actions. I just wish I had brought more along with me.

The Shwenandaw Kyaung, the Golden Palace Monastery, is a truly magnificent structure with its nineteenth century woodcarvings. Here, the novice monks peer curiously through doorways as some Burmese university students strike up conversation with Iew and I in English. They are only too keen to converse: a trait I have found to my delight already on so many occasions.

Sagaing, former capital of upper Burma, lies about twenty kilometres south–west of Mandalay. We pass through wonderful countryside and cross, incredibly, the only bridge spanning the Irrawaddy. Built by the British, the Ava Bridge has been the target of several insurgency groups, so taking photographs is forbidden.

The contradictory view of Sagaing.

There couldn't be a more beautiful place to pass the early evening than Sagaing. As the bus pulls up, hordes of young girls cascade on us yelling 'mingala baa'. They offer flowers and accompany us up to the Pa Ba Gyaung Monastery. The views here of the river and surrounding country-side, dotted with magnificent stupas, are quite breathtaking. I walk away to be alone and gaze in awe at the country below, stretching far away. At a peaceful moment like this, it is scarcely credible that Sagaing itself was witness to some of the worst scenes of brutality during the 1988 uprisings.

Friday, 16th November:
Mist swirls around the Irrawaddy. For a while you believe it's going to be a cool day. But you've been deceived again. Is it ever cool in Mandalay? We wait by the banks of the great river for the boat to take us to Mingun, some one and a half hours away. As tourists we are lucky — our vessel has an engine. Those without are hauled upstream by some unfortunate person. At least they escape the deafening racket of the Burmese engine.

Mingun is famous for housing the largest uncracked bell in the world — Moscow's is larger, but flawed. You can actually crawl underneath and peer inside — and pray that nobody rings it. It's vast: almost four metres high and weighing eighty-five tons. There's no chance of it being copied anywhere else in the world: for the craftsman who designed and con-structed it was promptly executed afterwards. That's one way of preventing forgery, I suppose.

Not far away stands a second potential entry into the *Guinness Book of Records*: the world's largest pile of bricks. This vast stone slab was the brainchild of the mad King Bodawpaya (one of Rin's distant cousins, perhaps?). Now King Bodawpaya believed he was Buddha reincarnated and, in 1790, decided to build the largest pagoda in the world. It took seven years to construct — by which time most of the workers were dead and, worse for the King, finances were at a low ebb. The whole plan was a total fiasco and had a devastating effect on local society. Villagers fled to escape being called upon to continue the construction.

Mingun Pagoda.

King Bodawpaya was, indeed, a nutter. He had all his rivals massacred, including the royal family. And his way of meting out punishment to someone he felt had betrayed him was to destroy everything in the village — men, women, animals, trees, plants. Oh, I forgot to mention — the bell was Bodawpaya's idea too.

The Mingun Pagoda is an extraordinary sight: in 1838 an earthquake struck and part of the structure collapsed. Today you can still see a huge fissure in the giant slab. It's really quite awesome. As we wander round in the scorching heat, two kids tag on behind, clad in mini 'longyi' and wearing two large circles of what appears to be chalk on their faces. In fact it is 'thanakha' and is made from the bark of a tree.

Monsieur, Madame and Iew have gone to explore another temple. I prefer to sit outside and wait: I'm put off by the sign at the entrance which reads: 'FOOT WEARING IS STRICTLY PROHIBITED'. I don't fancy removing my feet in this heat. So I strike up conversation with some students who are just strolling about aimlessly. Theirs is an all too familiar tale: nothing to do since 'The Old Man' (Ne Win) shut the universities. It's a depressing story; they appear cheerful but deep within there is resentment and frustration.

The return journey to Mandalay is a joy for the boat 'draggers': downstream they don't have to pull. I decide to forego lunch at the hotel and ask the guide to recommend an 'authentic' Burmese restaurant, which is a short ride away by cyclo (or 'sidecar', as the Burmese call them). Since Iew is readily mistaken for a Shan, I appear to be the sole foreigner and this causes great diversion. The food is no better than at the hotel: the meat is tough and cold, and has obviously been hanging around all day. The curry sauce is swimming in grease and I just know I'm going to get the 'squits'. And sure enough, not one hour later, I am firmly wedged in what could well qualify for Burma's third entry in the *Guinness Book of Records*: the world's foulest and most overpriced water–closet.

To fully explore Mandalay, there is no finer way than to take a horsecart. So Monsieur (who could barely scramble inside), Madame, fussing and clucking, Iew and I set off around town. It was a wonderful evening. And after the French couple had retired, we sat on the pavement outside the hotel, chatting with the cyclo drivers and any passers–by who happened to stop. And so many did, just to look or say 'hello'. Kids, too, appeared from nowhere, catching beetles for their supper. Or maybe just for a snack. Truly an extraordinary land.

Saturday, 17th November:
On the road to Mandalay — to the airport. And I've only seen one flying fish: it popped up on the way to Mingun. But I've seen much, much more. And learned a great deal too. I leave not downhearted with the plight of the country, but elated with having discovered a new land. A land so much more genuine than the gems it has for sale, more genuine, too, than its seedy, flawed, commercialized neighbour. A land stood still; a land where frustration and delight go hand in hand. A land where every step and every glance have the capacity to thrill. A land of marvels. And what about my customs declaration form? Lost in the morning mist of the Irrawaddy, for all I know.

The contrast of Chiang Mai: the evening is spent dancing away at the Bubble Disco. In Mandalay, a mere hour's flight from here, they are dining on locusts, on beetles caught in the city streets and puffing away on cheroots. And wondering, no doubt, when it'll all change for the better. Better? Bubble Disco at the Pornping Hotel: I'm not so sure.

Sunday, 18th November:
What could be more enjoyable than a Sunday in Lamphun? John is still hard at work on his book *Touring Northern Thailand* and we hop in the jeep to check up on the Mae Sa valley. Everything appears to be where it ought. So it's time to say 'sawatdee': we're off to Bangkok in the morning. Will John and Rin still be together when I come back someday? (Was she *ever* together?) Will peace return to '271 Pa Hew Soi 2 Moo 7'?

Monday, 19th November:
The heat and stench of the Thai capital have encouraged me to head back to Europe and to Vienna. After all my days in this madhouse, I'm just another foolish 'farang'. Reason: I'm readily persuaded to fly, first class, on Royal Jordanian, via Amman. Just thirty thousand two hundred and fifty-five baht, discounted *specially* for me. *"No probrem fly to Gulf?"* I naively inquire. *"Sure, sir, no worry, no probrem."* No, not for thirty thousand two hundred and fifty-five baht, cash.

Thursday, 22nd November:
Iew returns to his village. I prepare myself for the outbreak of war in Amman by sinking a few Singhas, and learn later of the Bangkok Airways Dash 8 which crashed at Ko Samui yesterday. Some consolation. Pass me another Singha.

Or maybe a Maekhong. My flight doesn't leave until a quarter past four in the morning, which gives me just enough time to find a copy of a Tax Clearance Certificate. Now there must be one in Patpong somewhere.

My nightmare journey to Vienna took in Bangkok, Calcutta, a night in the Amman Airport Hotel (missed connection but no war yet) and much abuse from the Royal Jordanian staff (male). What would I have given to be sitting on the verandah of the Thiripyitsaya Hotel, overlooking the Irrawaddy River, downing a few Mandalay beers? Certainly thirty thousand two hundred and fifty-five baht.

PART THREE

Isaan, Laos, Sumatra, Thailand . . . and Home

I left the UK on 3rd January 1991 and arrived in Bangkok the following day. My intention this time: to travel much further into 'Isaan', the North–East of Thailand, Iew's homeland. And, if possible, to cross the Mekhong River into Laos. And there, once more, to experience a country cut off from the West.

After four days in Bangkok, Iew and I flew up to Chiang Mai. And that's where the story begins again.

Monday, 7th January:
I forsake the delights of Chiang Mai's guest houses to stay at a newly built condominium with the very Thai name of 'City House Condo'. The owner, delighted to meet a 'farang', invites us to drink Maekhong with him. It would cause offence to refuse, so I am obliged to sit and suffer baby English for the evening.

Later other travellers show up — will they relieve the boredom? One is an American who is paying his first visit to the Kingdom. Curious thing: he has studied Thai at university in the States and speaks the language fluently. Yet he knows nothing of the culture or geography. Retire well tanked up — particularly as the owner wouldn't let me go until I'd downed a glass (for him, a half–bottle) of Johnny Walker Black Label. In such a status society, Black Label counts for quite a lot. He staggers off: he tells me he will drive to his home, a few kilometres away. Politely I inquire whether that's wise.
"You think me mao?" he asks.
"Nit noy."
"No probrem for me."
That could explain the high death–rate on the roads. I ask whether they have a breathalyser test in Thailand.
"Maybe," he replies. *"But nobody fail."* Oh, Thai repartee . . . in any case, the only time the police stop cars is at the end of each month when their pay packet is almost empty. And thus I bade him good–night . . . and *'chohk dee'*.

Tuesday, 8th January:
Yet again there are no seats available to Mae Hong Son. I doubt now I'll ever make it there. So instead it's off to Khon Kaen on Friday and the start of the 'Isaan' adventure.

Thursday, 10th January:
Retrace our steps on the wonderful road to Lamphun. John's book is still nearing completion and he has departed for Chiang Rai — with Rin. Topsy–turvy. Rin's mother entertains us briefly — leaving the fish alone for a while — before we set off for one of the real delights of Northern Thailand — Wat Prathat Haripunchai. Founded in 897, this magnificent royal monastery is almost as stunning as the Burmese temples. And indeed there is very much a Burmese feel to the buildings: the fifty–metre high gold–topped chedi is quite breathtaking.

Iew going to the dogs?

I stroll around the temple while Iew has his fortune read. The Thais are a very superstitious race: they seek inspiration and advice from fortune–tellers and palm–readers and place strong credence in the pieces of paper they receive at the temple. You make a donation, are given a number and then take a sheet of paper which corresponds to that number. Often they have a translation in English — obviously done by the same person who translates Thai restaurant menus. As with western horoscopes, they rely heavily on sweeping generalisations: *"You will be lucky in love and money"* or *"You will meet a rich, handsome fool of a 'farang' who wants to give you all his cash"* and other such likely tales. Judging by his smile, Iew has got a 'result'.

From Lamphun we take a 'songthaew' to Pasang, about twelve kilometres south–west. Here, at the top of what appears to be almost as many steps as up Mandalay Hill, lies a temple with a quite unpronounceable name. It's scorching hot and I am reluctant to climb. Iew, being from 'Isaan', refuses point blank. He settles down to read a bloodthirsty Thai paper (featuring the latest victims of aggrieved Thai men, wives who've cut off their unfaithful husbands' willies and demented lorry–drivers) with a 'Splite' ('Sprite' by any other name). I climb the steps wearily: Thai novice monks pass me on the steps and smile. I'm sure they think me a crazy 'farang'. It's a steaming, hazy day and the view, alas, is disappointing. How I wished I was sitting in the shade down below with a 'Gleen Spot'.

Friday, 11th January:
The Thai Airways ATR 72 touches down quite smoothly at Khon Kaen Airport. We are in the heart of 'Isaan', the very core of Thailand. I had been to the North–East before — to Nakhon Phanom last year — but that was only for a cursory glance.

Other than Chiang Mai, I have yet to come across a Thai town that offers anything — at least from an architectural point of view. Chiang Rai, Nan, Phitsanulok — they are all ugly 'shoeboxes'. And Khon Kaen, alas, is no exception. The town has no charm, no character — but, thank God, no 'farangs'. Here you find the true spirit of Thailand, the real warmth, the genuine smile. Tourism — and with it commercialism, a dying culture and tradition — has yet to come to 'Isaan' (if indeed it ever will) and the area has been spared to a large extent the hassles and rip–offs that are so much a part of Bangkok, Pattaya, Chiang Mai and Phuket. 'Isaan' cannot offer beaches, nor hilltribes, but what it does offer is a sincereness that does not exist elsewhere. Poverty and hardship abound — the people have scarcely benefited from the economic boom — and life carries on much as before. The farmers farm, praying for a decent rainfall, the weavers weave and the tradesmen ply their trade along the Mekhong River. They speak 'Isaan' — and Lao — and eat 'sticky' rice, 'somtam', 'larb' and 'gai yang'. They catch giant catfish, race boats on the Mekhong, round–up elephants and partake in some of the most enjoyable festivals in the Kingdom. There are no five–star hotels or high–class restaurants, no Patpongs, no floating markets and no rose gardens. Just normal, industrious people trying to eke out a living. Just 'Isaan'.

Iew has suddenly remembered that his grandmother, whom he hasn't seen for at least fifteen years, lives in a village near Khon Kaen. So he hops into a 'tuk–tuk' for what is sure to be an unemotional Thai reunion. He returns a few hours later surprisingly elated. He wants me to meet her tomorrow.

Saturday, 12th January:
His grandmother lives in a village called Ban Nong Hai, about four kilometres out of town. We stock up with gifts for her — including 'O–one–teen' ('Ovaltine') — which is to be expected of a visitor. As a 'farang', I am automatically granted superior status and must conduct myself accordingly.

Ban Nong Hai has probably never seen another 'farang' before. It is a rather nondescript place, dusty and without character. As a mark of respect I 'wai' Iew's grandmother. The wooden house is like any other in Thailand with a corrugated iron roof and a television aerial. They sit underneath, chatting and eating.

There is far more of a community spirit in Thai villages than in English suburban ones. They are more like large families, though not always happy ones. They eat and drink together, work together and do a large amount of talking together. The families themselves are much more tightly knit, too: while the mothers and fathers are at work in the fields, the grandparents look after the young children. In turn, the children will take care of their older relations when the time comes. And though there is a tendency in 'Isaan' for the men to venture south to Bangkok to earn money — often as 'tuk–tuk' drivers — and for the young women to seek employment in factories and brothels, there are still others to fulfil their duty for them. In England, of course, most cannot wait for the moment to flee the nest and to shirk all responsibilities. The thought of having to look after relatives who are too infirm to care for themselves is anathema to most of us. Far easier to shove them in a home and forget about them. The family unit barely exists any more. But for the Thais 'taking care' is a vital part of everyday life. And don't think that 'farangs' are immune from this attitude: as many a bar–girl has said to her customer *"Marry me, you marry my family"*.

Iew's grandmother is, according to him, in her nineties (I'm sceptical), yet remains graceful and charming. We can barely communicate so we sit and drink. I am offered a Thai dessert, which is sickeningly sweet (as most are) but which I pretend to enjoy. Two girls are weaving reed mats next to me: they will sell them on and earn just about enough to survive. But that's what life here is about — survival, living from day to day. Nobody gets rich, few starve: the villagers see that there is enough food to go round. Rice, that is. For the Thais, to eat is to eat rice — 'gin kao', whether it be 'kao suay' (steamed rice) or, throughout the North–East, 'kao niaow' ('sticky' rice). 'Sticky' rice has become something of a joke in Thailand — those from the Central Plains of Bangkok, and from the South taunt the 'sticky' rice eaters. 'Sticky' rice, they say, makes your nose short and stubby (a reference to the fact that many 'Isaaners' have such noses) and makes you sleepy. Their reputation for laziness is no more deserved than it is for Thais elsewhere in the Kingdom.

A cousin — how often I've heard that word used in a Thai community — shows me round. He speaks no English and gabbles to me in Thai, most of which I cannot understand. Yet even if I explain to him that I can't follow what he's saying, he continues talking . . . and talking. Funny, people often don't grasp the fact that you're foreign and can't comprehend. So I smile and nod and follow him. He shows me a rice mill — if that's what they're called — where the rice goes in one end and comes out another, looking slightly different. Not 'sticky' rice, that's for sure. Then more weavers: two pretty girls hard at work. It doesn't take much of an imagination to picture them a few hundred miles south sporting just a bathing costume and doing extraordinary things with ping–pong balls. Cock–fighting. More like fighting over them, I suppose. But that's what I stumbled upon next. And then, by chance, a wedding party 'Isaan'–style.

Imagine falling perchance upon a marriage at home — clad only in T–shirt and shorts. What would the host say? *"Get the f**k out of here, you're gate-crashing."* If you were lucky. But in the North–East, you are an honoured guest, the very surprise of your arrival eliciting whoops of delight. Bottles of Maekhong and cans of Singha appear from nowhere, plates of 'larb' and 'somtam' (accompanied of course by 'sticky' rice) materialise spontaneously. The girls vie desperately for attention: a multitude of dishes is placed before me. I have to sample each and every one. More Maekhongs, more Singhas. Hospitality that could never be found in the West.

And yet it all becomes too oppressive. The attention is wearing. The men grow ever more intoxicated, the girls more pushy. Marriage proposals are bandied about. It's time to leave.

Alcohol effects extraordinary transformations in the Thai character. Aggression, simmering just below the surface, readily reveals itself, along with dramatic mood swings, hostility and brutality. Despite its smiling image, Thai society is very violent and quite incredibly bloodthirsty. The murder rate is high — over eight thousand a year — and the Thai fascination with all things gory is legendary. They have ferocious tempers when roused — maybe because they spend much of the time suppressing them (the 'mai ben lai' syndrome again). And there are those who consider Thai society one of the most hypocritical in the world. There is certainly plenty of evidence for that if, for example, you consider the murder statistics, the number of monks carrying Sony Walkmans (not to mention HIV infection), and the scandal of the high–ranking monk who allegedly impregnated a woman. That one has run and run in the Thai press. And how do they excuse the fact that Buddhists shouldn't kill animals? *"Oh, I was just sitting by the sea with a net in my hand trying to stop the fish from drowning when this stupid pomfret swam right into it. I took the net out of the water to get a better look and it just died on the beach. So I fried it in the wok that I just happened to have with me and ate it."* More serious, of course, was the treatment meted out by the Thai border patrols to the Cambodian refugees, who had fled from the horrors of Pol Pot in the summer of 1979. They were sent back forthwith to face almost certain death.

And, to bring the hypocrisy right up to date, what about a certain Thai company's plan to construct a casino on Burmese soil in the 'Golden Triangle'? Rumours about this bizarre scheme have been circulating for some time: it is alleged that a Thai enterprise called Withawat International Company, owned, surprise, surprise, by a Thai politician, is investing no less than three million baht to build the so–called 'Paradise Resort' on more than thirteen hundred acres of Burmese land. Paradise for whom? Not for the Burmese people, but for the hordes of 'farangs' who can enjoy the delights of an eighteen hole golf course, a shopping centre, a four hundred room hotel, hospital, and a hovercraft docking area. And . . . a casino.

Now gambling, of course, is illegal in Thailand, as indeed it is in neigh-bouring Burma. But let's turn a blind eye . . . and get very rich instead. For the contract is a thirty–year concession, affording the project owner exclu-sive rights over the concessioned area. The Thai government can do nothing about it (or doesn't want to) and as for the Burmese military, well they're benefiting to the tune of thirty million US dollars in rental fees during the thirty–year period. And all tax–free for the first eight years. No wonder in Burma they frown upon the path Thailand is pursuing.

Sunday, 13th January:
Third class train compartment to Nong Khai. Dusty.

Not long ago Nong Khai — with its magnificent location by the river — must have been a wonderful spot, bereft of tourists. Now there are guest houses popping up everywhere — with original names like 'Mekhong Guest House'. For Nong Khai (which, according to the Thai pronunciation, could actually mean 'chicken thigh') is the major land (or rather water) crossing into Laos, the former French colony which once again is opening its doors to hordes of backpackers. And the merchants of Nong Khai province aren't going to lose out on this vast influx of 'farangs'. They can get you your visa for anything up to two thousand five hundred baht (it costs them just three hundred baht at the Lao Embassy in Bangkok), organ-ise your accommodation: indeed Nong Khai is rapidly becoming a mini Chiang Mai.

The town itself is not as ugly as many, with a good deal of greenery and not too many 'shoeboxes'. Most interest surrounds the border crossing point where 'farangs' without Lao visas hang around watching the traffic come and go across the Mekhong. Thais don't need visas to cross the river — as long as they come back the same day — and they can stay for three days if they obtain a permit from the authorities. The trade between the two contrasting countries continues all the while.

If you've obtained your visa in Bangkok, you can either fly into Vientiane by Thai Airways or, for the very brave, by Lao Aviation. Failing that, you must cross from Nong Khai to the Laotian town Tha Deua by boat — and make sure you tell the travel agent which way you're going as the Lao Embassy stamp it in your passport. Laos is slowly becoming more accessible again, after very much a stop–stop approach to tourism. Indeed they've now set up a company at Bokaew, across the Mekhong from Chiang Khong in Chiang Rai province, to promote a new tourist route. So who knows what will happen in a few years' time.

Thais consider Laos as something of a joke, in the same way as the French deride the Belgians. They can't understand why anyone could possibly want to visit a country like that, but then the Thais themselves have always been short–sighted in this respect. Why go to 'Lao' when you have beaches, temples, great food and whores aplenty in Thailand? Maybe to explore a land which is untainted by tourism (it has no rail network) and commercialism, and which has managed, like its neighbour Burma, to preserve its culture. In that connexion, the Laotian government has got it right. But, of course, Laos is a desperately poor country with an average yearly income per person of a little over a hundred dollars, so you can't have it both ways.

In the same way Thais regard 'Isaan', so 'Isaaners' regard Laos. And Iew is no exception. There is no interest whatsoever, merely scorn. But for me, Laos is a most mysterious land about which we learn little in the West. And it is beckoning now.

Monday, 14th January:
I pay two thousand three hundred baht for my visa which takes five days to process. So plenty of time to relax by the Mekhong, watch the world go by and to . . . meet an Englishman from Stoke. A most weird character too. A perfect candidate for 'What's My Line?': he has been trying to export Lao coffee to Australia for three years — hitherto without success. But he is convinced it's a potential money–spinner. I wasn't sure where he got his finances to fund his three year (abortive) venture — several flights from Australia to Bangkok, then up to Nong Khai and onward into Laos. I suspect he had a few other little schemes.

Nong Khai boasts some beautiful temples, though that's not how you'd describe Wat Kaek. Weird, eerie, like something out of Disneyland. It's a Hindu–Buddhist shrine with all manner of grotesque figures: snakes, rats . . . a strange sight.

I wonder if snakes and rats were what the translator had in mind when he worked on the menu at one of the guest houses in town: 'Morning glory inferno', 'Eight Angels' and 'Three Vikings in Thai style' are all available. Little wonder the restaurant is deserted.

Tuesday, 15th January:
Each evening, at six pm, the *Bangkok Post* arrives from the capital; then the 'farangs' rush to catch up on the impending war, which seems so very far away. And it is the Thais who are completely transfixed as they hover around every available TV set, engrossed, ecstatic, bemused. They've learnt a new word, too. It's 'Saddam': *"Saddam, mai dee. Saddam bad man."* Running down 'Saddam' has become 'sanuk', and good business for vendors of Saddam T-shirts.

I take to the Mekhong instead, and travel sixteen kilometres east, lunching in a remote village on 'Isaan' hospitality and a noodle soup of pork and squid.

Thursday, 17th January:
By now I feel I know Nong Khai quite well. I am becoming restless. Maybe it would have been wiser to have got the visa in Bangkok. Unless you're a dope-smoking backpacker with no cares in the world, there's sod all to do here.

Temples, temples and more temples. Wat Sisaket, Wat Pochai, wat, wat, wat. And all the monks want to talk, and talk. The same questions: *"Where you come from? Where you going? How long you stay? What's your name? How old you?"* And end of conversation.

Perhaps in their spare time they translate the local menus:
   'Lucky duck' — the duck probably disagrees.
   'Stewed trionyx' — not in my dictionary.
   'Fall beef' — an autumn speciality?
   'Stewed abalone with three things'. What 'things'?
   'Fried rice-birds'.
   'Five things soup in fire-pan' — those strange 'things' again.

Friday, 18th January:
Iew and I — or rather just I — had hoped to be crossing the Mekhong today, but *"Sorry, visa not come. Mai ben lai. Come tomorrow for sure,"* the travel agent's bluster. So another night in 'Isaan's' 'City of Angels' — and 'Vikings'.

Saturday, 19th January:
Laos is calling — Tax Clearance Certificate or no. A Thai official demands an eight hundred baht fine from Iew: I inquire why — Iew replies :
   "You pay eight hundred baht for me or me cannot go Lao."

"Why?"

"You must pay. Man say pay, so pay for me now." He refuses to elucidate. Later he tells me that they wouldn't have allowed him in if I hadn't paid. They had seen a Thai travelling with a 'rich farang' and, without having planned it, promptly milked the foreigner of a quick seventeen pounds.

And I was always told that the Thais didn't have a word for corruption. To them, it was a Western disease known simply as 'collupshun'. I suppose they didn't need to define it — if they kept on doing it, they couldn't forget it.

I am allowed to stay two weeks, Iew three days. But he's delighted about that. I always get the impression that Thais are ashamed about Laos, as if it's some huge carbuncle on the side of their Kingdom. The Lao People's Democratic Republic, now there's a misnomer: isolated, undeveloped, undisturbed, unknown, that's Laos. Quite unlike its ebullient, brash neighbour in most respects, Laos also has slightly less of a Buddhist influence: only about half the population follow Theravada Buddhism. Their spiritual home is Luang Prabang, about thirty-five minutes by Antonov 24, and not the so–called capital Vientiane, a dusty, ugly place — not unlike many Northern or North–Eastern Thai towns. Here the French influence is very much apparent — in the architecture, the French–style boulevards and baguettes for sale in the markets. But there's little charm, little humour; it's rather a sad, depressing place. You feel the people are waiting for something exciting to happen. Waiting, perhaps, for Thailand.

Once, the Anou Hotel might have been quite reasonable; now it's run–down with very much an Eastern European feel to it: amorphous, indifferent and characterless. And at three hundred baht — without a loo — it's hardly a bargain. Settle up in dollars or baht, but not kip, unless you've got a fork–lift truck to transport the bundles around with you.

French restaurants and a few temples are all Vientiane has to offer: unless of course you speak Lao or have an interest in the government propaganda that is broadcast on the street corners early in the morning and evening.

Just my luck: my interpreting skills (?) are going to be called into action once again. I have teamed up with a young Parisian couple (Christian — bald, for some reason — and Michelle) who speak little English. Thankfully they're not a bit like Monsieur and Madame — for a start they're half their age. And Christian is constantly looking for dope — now that's not at all like Monsieur. We're off to Luang Prabang together on Wednesday.

At least the French did one good thing for Vientiane: they left their cuisine. Le Souriya is a marvellous restaurant, apparently owned by a Lao princess (though I didn't see any of the trappings of royalty). Pâté, filet de porc, salade verte, bouteille de vin rouge . . . 'sairp lai', as they say in Laos.

Sunday, 20th January:
The English coffee exporter is cycling through Vientiane. He obviously hasn't struck it rich yet. He accompanies me to the market, pointing out all the tremendous bargains to be had. The only one who's 'had' is me: he encourages me to buy some Cambodian riel notes. *"You'll get a good price for them at home,"* he assures me — a good return for my £5.40. Yes, and Mekhong catfish will go miaow.

At the end of Thanon Lan Xang lies a strange monument: half Arc de Triomphe, half Laotian. It's called the Pratuxai, which sort of means 'Arch of Triumph' — that's original. It was constructed in 1969 and is nothing like as grand as its Parisian relative: still, you get a great view of Vientiane and the surrounding areas from the top.

Monday, 21st January:
Iew leaves at seven am: the wailing from the loudspeakers just outside the Anou serves as a perfect alarm–clock.

There is little tourist infrastructure in Laos: most areas are out of bounds. Of the seventeen provinces, only Vientiane, Luang Prabang, Xieng Khwang (the Plain of Jars), Savannakhet and Champasak (Pakse) are at all accessible. And for all of these you have to go via Lao Tourism — the state–run travel office, not unlike Myanmar Travel and Tours. The mark–ups are enormous — a three–day trip to Luang Prabang costs two hundred and twenty-three dollars, double the average yearly income of a Laotian, who'd pay around six dollars for a flight to Luang Prabang. We pay over thirty.

Tuesday, 22nd January:
Wat Sisaket, the oldest temple remaining in Vientiane, dates back to just 1818, and Wat Phra Keo (no longer a temple but a museum), can compete with some of the temples over the border. Surrounded by a garden, Wat Phra Keo — temple of the 'jewel Buddha image' — is a tranquil, relaxing place. Sit and enjoy the peace and solitude.

Vientiane's — and indeed Laos' — most hallowed monument is That Luang, constructed in 1566 over an older stupa which is supposed to contain one of Buddha's chest bones. How many *did* he have? And what swine kept stealing them? That Luang is disappointing: it's deserted and nothing like as striking as some of the Burmese pagodas. And, so different from Thailand, too: just one lonely 'tuk–tuk' waits under the tree to take the sole 'farang' home. Yes, Vientiane is a town going nowhere, and there's not much charm or spontaneity amongst the people.

Wednesday, 23rd January:
Wattay Airport has a very Asian feel to it — more Calcutta than Changi. Hustle and bustle and no information. Queue–jumpers and chickens. And no guide. The flight, originally scheduled for 'early afternoon' had been put forward — now there's a turn–up — to ten o'clock in the morning. Maybe the Lao Tourism guide wasn't aware of this. Everyone seems to check in at the same desk anyway, so what the hell. The guide eventually appears. We are immediately sent to the front of the queue — being a foreigner some- times has its advantages — and actually allocated seat numbers.

From the runway comes the fearsome sound of Lao Aviation Antonovs, Mi–8 helicopters and an Aeroflot Tupolev warming up their engines. What a racket. I sneak a photo, half expecting to be led away by a Lao official. But no one notices.

Air conditioning, Lao-style . . .

Now I am not a good flier and the sight of the ancient Antonov 24 doesn't do much for my morale. There is no safety instruction card — by tradition the first thing I must read when I sit down — no safety announcements, no *'cabin crew doors to automatic and cross check'* and no pretty ladies demonstrating seatbelts, life–jackets and oxygen masks. Instead there's a deafening din, a cool towel, a chewy sweet and a cup of warm Coke. I am right at the front with the French couple on the other side of the aisle. But I don't see much of them because no sooner have we taken off than billows of smoke cascade down, enshrouding the entire seating compartment like some early–morning alpine mist.

A mere thirty-five minutes later the AN 24 touches down at Luang Prabang airstrip. As far as I can make out, peering through the smoke, the approach — over mountainous terrain — must be quite spectacular and I am at once reminded of the splendour of Pagan.

Located at the confluence of the mighty Mekhong and the Nam Khan Rivers, Luang Prabang is a sleepy town. Once the royal capital — that was way back in 1353 — it is very much the cultural and religious centre of Laos. Hilltribe villagers in black costumes mingle with Laotians: there are no foreigners anywhere to be seen. I stare at the locals and they stare back and I wonder who is the more intrigued.

There are striking similarities with Pagan: the mountains, the river, the breathtaking scenery. The charm and fascination of the elders, the smiling innocence of the children, the tranquility of the temples. I lose track of their names: Phu Si, Mai, That Luang, Visoun. But one I recall vividly — Wat Xieng Thong. For this magnificent structure — the Golden City Temple — built over five hundred years ago could vie with anything in Pagan. Mesmerizing.

Colonialism: how it has left its mark on Laos. The guide speaks French, and not a word of English. However, she persists in talking Lao (or Thai?) to me, as I foolishly mentioned that I could understand a few (a very few) words.

Foreigners are — for the moment anyway — only permitted to stay at two hotels: the Luang Prabang, which must be one of the very few in the land to boast a swimming pool, and the Phu Si. There are others (cheaper, too) which might accommodate you: it depends very much on the government's attitude to tourism. The Phu Si is not at all bad: it's a large, quiet place with friendly staff, some of whom are desperate to practise their English. I have to hold my tongue and exercise enormous patience as the receptionist attempts to give me directions to the post office in English: it's only round the corner (as I discovered later) but it takes him an age to get the words out.

There is a fair near the hotel and I stroll over. Of Laos' Buddhist neighbours, the nightlife takes after Burma rather than Thailand — in other words, practically nil. The fair, though, is abuzz with kids who are more than a little bemused to see a foreigner on their stamping–ground. They want me to take part: they have an old dart–board and they encourage me to throw a few darts. I know I'll make a fool of myself and thereby give them great amusement. So I chuck three darts: two miss completely and they are all delighted. I saunter off, pursued by several kids who are quite intrigued. I am like an untamed animal: they're not sure whether I might bite them, so they keep their distance. But when I buy some sweets and hand them out, their reluctance and uncertainty vanish and they are eager to approach. We cannot communicate but sweets and smiles suffice.

Thursday, 24th January:
Early mornings in Luang Prabang can be cool and refreshing — and mis-leading. By ten o'clock the sun is through and you can discard your sweater. I wander down to the market, surrounded by Laotians, Hmong and other hilltribe villagers. I am attracted to the silverware stalls, as indeed are the hilltribes who use the old coins to adorn their intricate costumes. Curiously, there are stacks of old rupees, some from the East India Company, among a myriad of other coins. They are supposed to be solid silver and are sold strictly be weight — though, of course, bartering is essential. There are many silver antiques — an old and well smoked opium pipe catches my eye (amongst other curiosities) which, after some good–natured haggling, I secure for a few kip.

The Royal Palace — former home of Laos' last King, Savang Vattana – boasts some extraordinary gifts from other monarchs and world leaders. It just goes to show: when you're in, you get teacups from Mao, presents from the King of Thailand and your flag is carried to the moon aboard the Apollo spacecraft. When you're out, you get despatched to Northern Laos and never heard of again — maybe to join B. Bumble and The Stingers (what-ever happened to them?) Such a fate befell King Savang Vattana, whose res-idence, like Imelda Marcos' shoes, is open to public viewing, gawping and aweing. There are some magnificent Buddha images, including the gold Prabang, brought from Angkor in the fourteenth century, which is eighty-three centimetres tall and weighs more than forty kilogrammes.

There are more statues of Buddha than of anyone else in the world — and over seven thousand of them stand in a cave about thirty kilometres by boat up the Mekhong. These are the Pak Ou caves: the lower ones, Tham Thing and Tham Phum, house the manifold images. It is a wonderful journey along the Mekhong: serene and relaxing with spectacular views of the mountains of Northern Laos. There is barely the sight of another boat on what at times must be a busy thoroughfare. Along the banks we pass Laotian women panning for gold and plants which look suspiciously like dope. The dope is on sale openly at the market in Vientiane, hanging up in bags at twenty baht (or the kip equivalent) a time. Finally we pass a rice–whisky distillery standing on the sandbanks. The stuff is potent and evil — you've got to knock it back in one go, it's no good sipping it. It really is one of the nastiest tasting drinks I've ever sampled. But, as with so many things in South–East Asia, you've got to taste, then smile . . . then grimace in private. Or you can do what I tried: don't swallow the stuff, hold it in your mouth and hope their attention is distracted by another sucker. Then turn your back and spit it out, unnoticed if possible. They call the stuff 'lao, lao': maybe they mean 'foul, foul'.

Wherever you go in Luang Prabang, the views are wonderful and the atmosphere so peaceful. From the hill Phu Si down to the town or just along the Mekhong. It's difficult to believe it's a neighbour of oh so brash Thailand.

Friday, 25th January:
Lao Aviation's reservation system is almost as curious as the air–conditioning on its antique Antonovs. If you're a politician you get first choice, if you're a visiting VIP second choice, if you're a tourist, you're third on the list and if you're a Laotian, no choice. The flight is never full for a high–ranking official, but it's just bad luck if you're an ordinary Lao citizen. There are seats on Sunday's flight to Vientiane, but no, the guide couldn't promise one to me because . . . well because someone else might require it. *"Who?"* I inquire.

. . . *and reservations, Lao-style.*

"Somebody," comes the curt reply.
"Somebody who?"
"Somebody maybe government."
"Well how many seats are available?"

"Depends." And so it goes on. Further discussion is pointless. Later she informs me that the mysterious official *is* travelling on Sunday and the plane is suddenly full. That's Asia.

I am steadily becoming a vegetarian — thanks to Luang Prabang's meat market. The stench is noxious, the sight putrid: the women sit all day fanning the flies off a chicken thigh as the midday sun sedately rots the merchandise. I haven't been able to eat for two days now and the thought of chicken fried rice — there isn't much else available at the hotel — makes my stomach turn.

A man could get forgotten in Luang Prabang, where life carries on seemingly untouched by the outside world. At times I wish that man were I.

That evening in Wat That, not far from the hotel, there is a fête. Food is handed out free — well, in return for a small donation to the temple — and Michelle and Christian (who partook at lunchtime) recommend I take a look. The cooking is handled by a group of Lao women, elegant despite the ordeal of preparing the food all day long under the Luang Prabang sun. With the thoughts of the market very much in my mind, I am reluctant to join in, but such is their persistency that in reality I have little choice. The food is cold and tasteless — and is accompanied by 'sticky' rice, of which I've grown quite tired. Once again, I feign enjoyment. Why do I always end up in these predicaments?

From the moment I set foot in the temple grounds, I am followed by a little kid who can hardly be more than six or seven years old. His clothes are torn and filthy and he has no shoes: he couldn't have had a wash for many days. He reminds me rather of the 'Artful Dodger' in *Oliver Twist*: mischievous, impish but so alluring. He steadfastly refuses to leave my side, but at no time does he beg for money. Maybe I do the wrong thing, but I clandestinely pass the waif a wad of notes: a beaming smile illuminates his face. Like the cat which got the cream . . . or the kip.

Saturday, 26th January:
Early morning by the Mekong: Luang Prabang is shrouded in an eerie mist. The merchants continue their business regardless: the road leading down to the river is bustling with activity. Assorted hilltribesmen mix with Laotians in their search for the day's provisions. Right by the banks of the Mekong, well worn wooden boats bob in the water in anticipation. All day long they traverse the muddy waters: bringing monks, novices, sellers. The far bank of the river is only just visible through the mist. What stood so clear yesterday is now but a memory. The mountains, the temples, the caves, all lurking in the haze.

To reach the river bank, I climb down some steps which in the rainy season are completely under water. The river rises by several metres, submerging everything in its path. Even the houses can't escape its wrath. Yet now it's hard to believe the Mekong can do all that: its serenity can be fatally deceptive. Many have been caught out by the currents.

A few kip secures my passage to the other side. For the monks and women with their big baskets full of vegetables and other wares, this is one of many, many crossings. For me it is an adventure, a mesmerizing journey across the Mekong which only now is giving up its morning secrets.

The banks of the Mekong are tremendously fertile and when the waters are low, support all kinds of crops. There are no steps on this side and I have to crawl up to the houses. There I am met by several curious children and an older guy who greets me to my utter surprise with *"Sprechen Sie Deutsch?"* He worked in East Germany, he tells me, in Dresden, in a factory. How distant it must seem from here — a remote village in Northern Laos.

A track leads through the village passing temples, caves and dwellings, some deserted and dilapidated, others still occupied. And everywhere I go I am followed by children, and at every house I am greeted with a *"sabai dee"*

The kids, giggling and shy, shadow my every move. I try talking to them in simple Thai but they don't respond, they only giggle all the more vociferously. I ask an older lady if there isn't any school for the children to attend, but she just looks back at me blankly. I make an attempt in French, but that elicits an identical response.

By midday the sun's rays are blazing down. The transformation from just three hours earlier is quite remarkable. There is an oppressive stillness about the place. I want to sit down and take in the majestic views of Luang Prabang, and in particular of Phu Si with its glinting pagoda. It is a world removed from my home. Supper later of soup, fried rice, chips, salad and a lemon juice: £1.13.

Sunday, 27th January:
I am on my way back to the hotel when I am distracted by music coming from nearby. Foolishly believing it to be the Luang Prabang disco, I follow the sounds, only to discover — as in Ban Nong Hai — it is a wedding party. I offer my apologies and make to walk away. But the host will have none of it and beckons me in. Again I make my excuses, but he is quite insistent. They clear a place for me in the front by the dance floor, put food and whisky on my table and, one by one, the girls — at first coy — ask me to dance. The party has clearly been going on some time and in true Lao fashion, most of the male guests are three–parts gone.

How easy conversation is with a pickled Laotian. You just smile and shake your head knowingly. And unlike the Thais, they don't seem to get at all pushy or truculent.

The band is well oiled too. But I'm not sure how much that influences the dancers. Maybe it's just that they aren't used to Laotian pop music: their sense of rhythm is quite extraordinary, like that of the girls in Chiang Mai's

Lao restaurant. I cannot turn down the ladies' repeated requests to dance, yet it is not easy with girls who will neither look you in the eye nor dance in time to the music. Each dance ends courteously with a 'wai'. And still no eye–contact and no rhythm.

Monday, 28th January:
At just before one pm, a taxi turns up at the hotel. I am returning to Vientiane: there are clearly no officials or VIPs waiting for today's flight.

The Lao Aviation Mekhong mist conceals most of the homeward journey.

Tuesday, 29th January:
The morning of my thirty-first birthday is largely spent in a broken–down 'tuk–tuk' on the road from Vientiane to Tha Deua. The twenty kilometre journey is punctuated by woeful spluttering sounds as the ailing 'tuk–tuk' chugs along until finally it cries enough. The driver, seemingly unconcerned that his major source of income is expiring beneath him, never stops smiling and shrugging his shoulders; he had pushed the 'tuk–tuk' beyond all reasonable limits and it had responded with a shudder, a stutter and a stall.

Three times it died, three times it was resurrected. And all through he never stopped smiling. It felt like the closing scenes of *Genevieve* as we staggered over the finishing line. We had made it not to London, nor Brighton — but to Tha Deua, the border crossing back into Thailand.

Over the Mekhong to Nong Khai; Nong Khai to Udon Thani. In Udon my birthday supper of 'Gheese omelette and Beek Stuyoneff'. And later the 'squits' 'Isaan'–style.

Thursday, 31st January:
The journey from Udon to Nakhon Phanom takes five and a half hours — including an hour's wait in Sakhon Nakhon. There is little of interest en route, except the fellow passengers. Even here, a 'farang' is quite a rarity. They stare at me, but not at all menacingly as the braver ones attempt to make conversation. They are intrigued by my 'Ray Ban' sunglasses which they ask to borrow and pass around: each one in turn tries them on and looks round vainly ('Thaily') for appreciation, and hopefully admiration.

On the opposite side of the bus a woman has a large basket perched precariously on her lap.
    "Arai na kup?" I inquire.
    "Macharm," comes the giggling reply.
    Tamarind. She tries her best to sell me some but I decline. So she gives me a few free: 'Isaan' hasn't yet gone the way of Bangkok.

Friday, 1st February:
Retrace my steps of last April as I take a 'songthaew' to Bannapho, Iew's village. He tells me I should pay seven baht — the driver insists it's ten — who said the influence of Bangkok hasn't yet rubbed off on 'Isaan'? Still I won't quibble over six pence.

None of the passengers in the 'songthaew' is going as far as Bannapho, so there's a good chance I won't remember where to get off. They are curious as to why a 'farang' is going to the village: one suggests it's because I have some dealings with the refugees (there is a large Lao camp in Bannapho). *"Friend me how in Bannapho,"* I explain in Thai–English, for they don't understand my 'Isaan'.

My stop, I think. I bash my ten baht coin against the side of the 'songthaew' in time–honoured fashion to inform the driver I wish to get off. He slams his foot down hard on the brakes and the pick-up comes to a screeching, dusty halt.

The village didn't seem this large on my first visit, and I don't have a clue where to go. Iew had told me to go up to the first person I saw and say *"Thanomsil bai nai?"* (which roughly translated means *"Thanomsil, where he go?"*). Thanomsil is Iew's real name: most Thais have nicknames, reflecting in some way their character or looks, for example 'moo' (pig) or 'lek' (little). I once even came across a baby called 'Snooker'. I didn't dare inquire why. As for 'Iew', well even Iew himself wasn't sure what it meant. How very Thai.

Imagine turning up at a bus–stop in Surbiton and asking *"Trevor, where he go?"* You'd certainly get some strange looks. Well maybe I was lucky, maybe I'd encountered yet another of Iew's many cousins. But no, this guy actually spoke English for, by coincidence, he was a Lao refugee — and a friend of Iew's. He was just going 'bai tio' — a pastime obviously handed on to the Laotians. He guided me to the house, which, for sure, I would never have found by myself; indeed I didn't even recognise it. They had been doing structural repairs. Piles of wood lay all around.

The bottles of whisky I brought for Iew's brothers — foolishly, as it happened, for they were teetotal (a hitherto unknown phenomenon in Thailand) — were swiftly consumed by the Lao refugee, his wife (who came along just for the 'sanuk') and various other uninvited guests. Of Iew's two brothers — Gonglian and Thanichai — one was out working, the other was dispatched on his 'motoby' to fetch Iew, whom, they said, was asleep in a house at the other end of the village. Iew had swiftly lapsed back into his 'Isaan' traditions.

Bannapho isn't a poor village by North-Eastern standards: there are television sets and motorbikes. Like so many of its type, Bannapho is a farming community where water buffalo are as bountiful as watermelon. They grow 'kao niaow', beans and cucumbers, wild cows and chickens wander about aimlessly. It's not an affluent lifestyle, but nobody starves. They are survivors who make the best of what they've got. They get by.

Saturday, 2nd February:
As That Luang is to Laos, so That Phanom — fifty kilomtres south of Nakhon Phanom — is to 'Isaan'. Quite simply, it is the most hallowed shrine in North–East Thailand. The central chedi, alas, collapsed in 1975

Next stop That Phanom.

after four days of torrential rain, though it was restored in 1979. It remains, nonetheless, a magnificent sight. Devout Thais will 'wai' That Phanom even if they are passengers shooting past at breakneck speed in a bus: alarmingly, the drivers sometimes do likewise.

Unfortunately I was just too late for the annual festival, when thousands of Buddhists converge on the temple. But, on what was a scorching hot day, it was still packed with monks, Thai tourists and the odd 'farang'.

Sunday, 3rd February:
About as far south from That Phanom as Nakhon Phanom is to the north lies Mukdahan. Overlooking the lethargic brown waters of the Mekhong, Mukdahan is situated directly opposite the Lao town of Savannakhet. And that's about all it has to offer. The accommodation is positively dreadful. The first two hotels I try — as mentioned in a well–known but inaccurate guide book — appear to have closed down, so the 'tuk–tuk' driver takes it upon himself to recommend another, surprisingly called the Mukhadan Hotel. *"Number one hotel in Mukdahan,"* so he says. I'd hate to see number two. Normally I'd be loath to accept guidance from a 'tuk–tuk' driver, but I had exhausted most possibilities and was losing patience. Since the guide–book described the remaining hotels as 'places to avoid', I didn't really have much choice.

Anyone thinking about writing a new guide to Thailand, please note: the Mukhadan Hotel (particularly at two hundred and fifty baht a room) *is* a place to avoid. Indeed so is the entire town. However, no sooner had we arrived than Iew remembered that his half–sister had a house somewhere in Mukdahan province. Not far from the town, he thought. He didn't have the exact address, but he did know the name of the village. And, fortunately, that of his half–sister, too.

'Not far' turns out to be an hour's ride by 'samlor'. It's the driver's lucky day: his 'tuk–tuk' hired for the afternoon by a *"farang"* who, as Iew likes to put it, *"have money too much"*.

I never thought that 'tuk–tuks' could reach such speeds. The man (well boy, really) drives with reckless abandon — get him a job in Bangkok at once. One leg hangs over the side . . . he's a maniac. I hold on for dear life, risking the occasional glimpse to see if we're still on the road. Is there a vehicle on the road left to overtake? Every now and then we come to a screeching halt and the driver jumps out either to have a pee or to ask directions, or, if he's quick, both. A sharp, sudden left–hand turn brings us into a village. Iew darts into the first house, only to reappear shortly after-wards. We then proceed further to another house. This time we all go in, remembering, of course, to remove our shoes. *"How sister you?"* I ask Thai–style. *"Maybe,"* he replies, 'farang'–style.

Evidently not, as a few moments later we are tearing off again down the path.
"Sister not here. She go away," Iew announces informatively.
"Go away where?"
"Not far."
'Not far, not far', 'maybe', 'no problem', 'don't worry' and, most infuri-
ating of all, 'up to me'. Or 'up to you'. How many 'farangs' have been
driven to the limits of despair and frustration by these phrases uttered by an
inscrutable Thai?

Deeper we venture into the village, where no 'farang' has ever
'tuk–tukked' before. The sandy lane becomes a dusty path. More inquiries,
then still further, into deepest Mukdahan. Finally, when we cannot
'tuk–tuk' any more, Iew proudly announces *"how sister me,"* leaving me
to wonder why Thais always form their sentences the wrong way round.
We are now at the very end of Ban Nong Weng Yai.

As before, there is no great welcome, no emotional reunion, no *"where
have you been all these years you selfish bastard?"* Just chat, bottles of
'Gleen Spot' and biscuits, courtesy of the *"farang who have money too
much"*. Iew's half–sister goes under the extraordinary name of Gairo Dtah,
which translated literally means 'glass eye' — not a replacement eye, but
rather a 'drinking glass eye'. Competition for baby 'Snooker', I guess.

Gairo Dtah has four charming young daughters, one of whom is so shy she
won't even show her face. They are a poor family, who have just enough to
get by. Their house is insubstantial: simply one room which serves as
bedroom, sitting room and kitchen. And then there are the chickens, which
spring up from below and run around madly, clucking incessantly. I
doubt the family ever gets much sleep. But then that's typical of life in a
village deep in 'Isaan' . . . marginally less comfortable than life in the
Mukdahan Hotel.

Monday, 4th February:
Now Ubon Ratchatani — the 'Royal Town of the Lotus Flower' (another
misnomer) — is altogether different from Mukdahan. An arduous bus
journey takes us into South–East 'Isaan' to Ubon which is built near the
banks of the Moun River, flowing eastwards into the Mekhong, where Laos
begins. South lies the war–torn land of Cambodia. Yet Ubon itself is
another of the concrete blocks that comprise the bulk of 'Isaan's' largest
towns: Ubon, Udon and Khon Kaen, whose rise began in the sixties as a
military base for the US and their bombing raids into Indochina.

Ubon has the best hotel in 'Isaan' — not that there's much competition.
The luxurious Pathumrat boasts a swimming pool, a disco, a snooker room
. . . and a giant rat lurking behind the reception desk. I am rather taken

aback by the sight of a large black rodent darting along the floor whilst I'm settling my account. I utter a muffled scream.

"Exqueue me sir, probrem with bin?" inquires the girl behind the desk as I stand open–mouthed.

"A rat," I stammer.

"Cat?"

"Rat, not cat."

"Yes hotel have cat. Brack cat."

In predictable Thai style, all the girls start giggling.

"That rat, not cat. Have long tail." I could see she couldn't understand the word 'tail'. So I got out my dictionary, found the Thai for 'tail' and pointed to it in the book: *"Hahng, hahng."* More titter. The conversation went no further. She was insistent it was a cat, I was convinced it was the biggest rat I'd ever set eyes on.

"Mai ben lai," I concluded, as I retired to the rat–free zone of my room. The 'PathumRAT', how aptly named.

Rat–free, perhaps, but not free from the mysterious menu–mistranslator who has struck the Pathumrat in stupendous style. Perhaps he graduated from Ubon University. Today's specials are:

From the drinks cabinet: 'Frest milk', 'green sport' and 'cok'. For hors d'oeuvres, 'miced soup', 'souured dausage salad', 'bacon bud egg' and 'Nic llowere salad'. For the main course, 'Pord chop and fegg', 'Strified poek', 'Steamed plajoke with plam sauce' and 'squid fried with ingredients for making a carry'. Or how about a selection of international favourites: 'Fried beef with stuff', 'Fried fish ball with long–been petty', 'Steamed dried snakeheads with pots and pans', 'duck's egg with ammonia' and 'Fried fomfart in gravy.' Rounded off with 'Pee pea in can'. And all 'Bound tightly with banana leaves'. We hope you 'velly enjoy'.

Tuesday, 5th February:

At the post office I am about to dispatch a package to Austria when a Thai gentleman in his fifties sidles up to me. Obviously keen to strike up conversation, he offers advice on how to wrap up and address the parcel. Such genuine friendliness and willingness to help is so common in 'Isaan' yet all too rare elsewhere. He is a lecturer at Ubon University and speaks excellent English. (Does he know the 'menu master'?). *"If you don't mind,"* he says, *"I would like to show you my University. You have time? Not far — you come on my motoby."* No time to worry about not accepting lifts from strangers, nor about crash helmets.

Now coming from a Thai, 'not far' normally has quite the opposite meaning but — happily for me, clinging on at the back — the University was just down the road. The lecturer was not from 'Isaan' himself — but from the south, from a town called Nakhon Si Thammarat. Yet he had all the charm and spontaneity of a local. He brought me coffee and insisted I shared lunch with his colleagues — a meal that was truly 'Isaan': 'somtam' ('pet mak mak'), 'gai yang' and 'kao niaow'. Alas none of the others could speak English — apart from the odd curiosity like *"Gary Lineker, Peter Beardsley, Steve Davies, Jimmy White,"* and that didn't really contribute much to the conversation. Yet we laughed and joked, and as I left — perched precariously on his 'motoby' — I knew, that for the final time on this journey, I was experiencing hospitality 'Isaan'–style. For tomorrow I intended to go south: to Penang and on to Sumatra.

Ubon to Bangkok — a laborious trip by train or bus — takes just an hour on the new Thai Airways BAe 146 'whisper jet'. And there's plenty of whispering at Don Muang Airport, too: with taxis in short supply tonight, touts mingle with passengers, discreetly offering their services. The domestic terminal is complete mayhem, despite newspaper reports that the War had emptied Bangkok. Empty? Not yet. They're all at the airport waiting to get out. And probably stuck in the traffic, too.

Whisper, whisper: *"You want taxi? Or you wait long time."* I ignore the first tout, and the second . . . and the third. My intention originally had been to stay at the Airport Hotel since I didn't feel it was worth the hassle of driving into Bangkok — and back out again — for the following day's flight to Penang. However I swiftly changed my mind when the obsequious girl at the hotel information desk quoted me three thousand two hundred baht for one night (at the Airport Hotel, that is). I requested the name of the cheapest hotel near the airport: *"You must go Golden Dragon Hotel, only six hundred baht. You booking?"* I thanked her for her advice, didn't make a booking and got led off by tout number four instead.

"Where you go, mister?" Here we go again.

"Golden Dragon Hotel. Near airport," I replied.

"I know good hotel, better than Golden Dragon. Not far. I take you." I sense I've had this kind of conversation before.

"No thank you. I stay Golden Dragon."

"You know Golden Dragon? Mai dee. Not good for you. I take you go good hotel. Sure, not bullshit." And despite insisting on being taken to the mysterious Golden Dragon Hotel (a place I must confess to never having heard of before), the taxi driver motored on regardless. 'Not far', on this occasion, was far enough for me. Forty minutes later we pulled in at the Mido Hotel.

I am in a foul mood. The room costs eight hundred and eighty–eight baht and I have a set–to with the receptionist who, for a change, speaks excellent English. So she should — she tells me she once worked in London, in High Street Kensington. She wants a thousand baht deposit and my passport. Never: I refuse and ask for the manager. I don't trust any Thai to retain my passport (especially overnight) and object violently to forking out a thousand baht. I offer to pay for the room in full now, but that doesn't satisfy her. A number of 'farangs', it would appear, have walked off with various items in their luggage. The argument is heated and very un–Thai.

The Mido Hotel brochure (I wonder, by the way, if Mido might be a cousin of the celebrated 'Fido Dido'?) says I am near the Victory Monument and a short drive from the airport. 'Short drive'? Nowhere in Bangkok is a 'short drive'. I console myself with this notice in my room — note the Thai–style punctuation (or rather lack of):

โรงแรมมิโด้

MIDO HOTEL

222 ถนนประดิพัทธ์ สะพานควาย

กทม. 10400

**NOTICE
TO OUR GUEST**

MIDO HOTEL HAVE A TAXI SERVICE, 24, HOUR'S AND EXPERIANCE
DRIVER ENGLISH SPEAKING AND GOOD GUIDE FOR SIGHTSEEING IN
BANGKOK OR UP COUNTRY WE TAKE CARE YOU LIKE OUR FAMILY
IF YOU FORGOT SOMTHING IN THE TAXI DO NOT LOSS, WE ARE
GARANTEE, TAXI DRIVER WILL BRING BACK TO YOU, WE INVITE
YOU TO USE OUR SERVICE YOU WILL LEAVE US FOR EVER'S
SAFETY FOR YOU LIKE AND YOU PROPETY
PLEASE CALL — 145
THANK YOU VERY MUCH
TRANSPORT FROM MANAGER

Mmm . . .

Wednesday, 6th February:
'WE TAKE CARE YOU LIKE OUR FAMILY': oh hapless family . . .
three hundred baht to the airport. I doubt many Thai families could afford
those prices. Since I have only bought two one–way tickets to Penang, we
can't check in . . . or rather Iew can't. Thais, so the girl at the check–in
desk informs me, are not allowed to travel out of the country without a
return ticket. That's to say, they are not free to leave the 'Land of the Free'
('Thai' means 'free') . . . so I have to return to the Thai Airways counter
and purchase a return for Iew — even if he doesn't intend to use it. The
woman, who sold me the two singles not half an hour before, is not pleased
to see me again. Funny, I was always told this was the land of charming,
smiling people. This Thai lady goes out of her way to irk me. I ask her for a
ticket for Penang–Bangkok. The conversation follows the all–too–common
surly Thai routine. Every time I suggest a day, she responds with:
"Sorry sir, all flights full."
"All full? Every day?"
"Yes sir, very busy. No seats."
How is it possible, I wonder, that every flight for the next few weeks —
let alone days — from Penang to Bangkok is full? I know she's just trying
to be difficult.
*"Right. I want a ticket for six months time. And don't tell me the flight's
full then."* She has no answer and reluctantly prints out the ticket whilst all
the time mumbling abuse about me to her Thai colleagues.

Checking–in is only one of a series of problems which confronts a Thai
citizen when he tries to leave the country. True, no Tax Clearance
Certificate, instead a one thousand baht 'Thai tax', a two hundred baht
airport tax and only then can he tackle passport control. The younger you
are, the harder it is to leave: the officials seem reluctant to let anyone
through. Iew is always treated with disdain by passport control — it appears
to me that they are trying their best to humiliate him and, if possible, not to
let him through. *"Where are you going, why are you going, how long will you
stay, how much money do you have?"* etc, etc: it's all so demeaning. Unless,
of course, you're on business, in the armed forces or in the government . . .
then they treat you with respect. This is one aspect of Thailand which really
gets to me. I am sure the passport officials are jealous that Iew can leave the
country and they can't.

Bangkok to Penang via Phuket. Both 'islands' — well they're not technically islands since they are attached to the mainland — have much in
common — top tourist attractions, great hotels, temples, drugs. Penang
isn't as sleazy as Phuket nor as commercial but it's got an air of authentic-
ity and of timelessness which its Thai sister certainly doesn't possess. You
pass Malays, Indians, Chinese — even Burmese who have arrived by boat
to work at the docks. It's a veritable ethnic hotchpotch.

Georgetown has a real Chinese feel to it, from the hotels with Chinese script to the restaurants serving outstanding fare with their high ceilings and fans whirring away, and their proprietors sitting around smoking and chatting. Yes, the Chinese hotels are a fascinating sight. One such — with a superb facade — is the Cathay Hotel, boasting the marvellously colonial address of '15 Leith Street'. It could be Kensington. Instead it's a wonderfully atmospheric place with a splendid interior. I don't know what the Thais have against Malaysia or the Chinese, but Iew immediately takes a dislike to Penang. *"Why?"* I inquire.

"No have tom yam." But is it really as simplistic as that?

Thursday, 7th February:
An Indian–looking man who speaks incomprehensible English takes us in his rickshaw for a tour of Georgetown. I'm never at ease in a rickshaw (or more correctly, a trishaw) — I feel like some colonial master. But it's the cheapest and most convenient way to explore the city: the museum (with its marvellously refreshing air–conditioning), Fort Cornwallis, the extraordinary Khoo Kongsi, the docks with the Burmese workers clad in their 'longyi' and — for me the most interesting — the Thai and Burmese temples. The Thai temple houses a huge reclining Buddha, thirty–three metres in length. At the Burmese temple on the other side of the road I talk to the abbot, who speaks fluent Thai having studied for some time in 'Isaan'. Iew and the monk chat away merrily as I admire the wonderful smiling Buddha.

Bangkok has the Oriental, Singapore Raffles, Rangoon the Strand and Penang . . . the Eastern and Oriental Hotel, knows as the 'E & O'. Built in 1885, the 'E & O' occupies a marvellous position by the sea: I sit outside and sip a cocktail, sampling the wonderful — if dated — colonial atmosphere. The service, alas, is surly and slow. Times ain't what they were.

Friday, 8th February:
Waiting for me outside the hotel is a scruffy, tattooed Malay guy who speaks good English. He tries to befriend me, invites me for a drink — I decline — and finally offers me some dope. Again I decline . . . *"You clever,"* he says, *"in Malaysia drugs mean death."* Then he disappears.

Iew and I check in for the flight to Medan, North Sumatra. A hand presses down on my shoulder. I turn round to see a policeman behind me. *"Excuse me, sir, I am a police officer. You won't mind coming with me downstairs, I wish to examine your luggage."* Iew doesn't understand what's going on — I do, but at times like this my mind goes blank. Is this just routine or could someone have planted something on me? I think back to the morning and the Malay guy: surely it was just a coincidence?

"You do realise, sir, that drug smuggling carries the death penalty in Malaysia?"

"I do." Guilty as charged.

"Then you won't have any objection to my searching your rucksack? Nor to my asking a few questions?"

"Go ahead." I try to remain cool and confident.

After posing the usual questions — name, address, age, occupation — we exchange pleasantries. He's quite an austere, aloof figure in his forties. How many smugglers has he caught before? How many are lingering in the notorious 'Death Row'? How many have already gone to the gallows?

"Just a routine search, you understand, Mr Greenwood. You can go now." I repack my rucksack and Iew his bag. I am still shaking by the time the flight is called an hour later. Iew is delighted to be leaving Penang. *"You think Indonesia have 'tom yam'?"* he asks plaintively. I haven't the heart to disappoint him.

"Maybe," I reply.

It's just a short hop from Penang to Medan . . . and then a few hour's wait at the airport for the onward flight to Padang. Medan Airport may be more modern than that of, say, Vientiane, the Lao capital, but check–in Indonesian–style is a treat with which even the Laotians can't compete. It's quite simple: locate your check–in desk, wave your ticket in the air, barge your way to the front, place your bag on the weighing–machine and your ticket on the top of the pile and yell *"I'm next."* For in Indonesia, it's certainly first come, first served. But with airlines like Garuda, Merpati, Sempati and Bouraq and aircraft such as Fokkers, DC–9s, Viscounts, Vanguards and 707s, even intrepid travellers think twice. Seven times I wander into the departure lounge, seven times the security staff fail to inspect my luggage. Who said something about a war?

Padang, the provincial capital of West Sumatra, is only fifty–five minutes by DC–9 from Medan. It is a wonderfully scenic approach to Tabing Airport, just north of the town, over mountains and low clouds. For the wet season is still upon us.

It seems that Iew and I are the only two people on the flight who don't know where they're going. Everyone else has someone to welcome them. The luggage is brought off the plane individually — it offers the handlers a chance of a few rupiah tip. And they don't leave you in any doubt: *"You have tip for me, sir?"* I refrain from saying *"Yes and it's running at Kempton this afternoon."* Instead I give one thousand rupiah.

Weird pointed rooves, enticing mountains and valleys, a wonderful verdancy, Padang wins me over almost at once. And the town's top hotel, which goes under the quaint, Italian–sounding name of the Mariani International, is quite extraordinary. It's eccentric, colonial, out of place . . . yet tranquil and hospitable. It offers de–luxe, first class and standard rooms: even the first class, exceptional by, say, Burmese or Lao standards, are only twelve pounds. The staff couldn't be friendlier, nor the dining–room emptier: and the menu . . . well most of the dishes aren't available. *"Prawns?"* — *"finis"*, *"beef?"* — *"finis"*, *"chicken?"* — that *"finis"* also. And, of course, they don't do pork. Still I'm told the noodles aren't bad.

Maybe it's the war, but there just aren't any foreigners around. As I stroll through the market, I am the object of a thousand stares, from curious eyes which peer and smile.

Saturday, 9th February:
Ah Bukittinggi — I may not be able to spell your name, but I couldn't forget you: layered rice–fields, waterfalls cascading into rivers, canyons, cinnamon trees and weird beetles which roll themselves up into impregnable balls. Just two hours from Padang and the air is cool and refreshing and the atmosphere oh so relaxed.

This is where the tourists have come: the Canadians, the Australians, the Germans and, of course, the Dutch. In some ways, Bukittinggi is the Sumatran version of Chiang Mai but very scaled down. Tours, tours, more tours . . . and mountains, 'traditional' houses and villages producing silverware. It's all there only without the cut and thrust of Thailand: here you just don't get the feeling you're being ripped off. For in Bukittinggi the smiles and welcomes *are* genuine.

Sunday, 10th February:
Woken at six am by what Iew thinks is a cat being strangled. If so, then it's got a deep and powerful voice. *"Not cat,"* I try to explain, *"Muslim."* He wasn't impressed. The wailing drones on remorselessly.

Bukittinggi is known as the home of the Minangkabau, a warm and hospitable race who have their own language and culture and whose society is matrilineal. That's to say, its the women who wear the trousers. Minangkabau, apparently, is Bahasa Indonesia for 'buffalo win' — 'minang' means win and 'kabau', buffalo. I think I was to discover why. One of the most striking features of the area is the wonderful architecture — the strange pointed rooves often marred, sadly, by the juxtaposition of rusty corrugated iron. The town itself seems quite out of place, with colonial–style horsecarts, a vast Clock Tower (built by the Dutch in 1827), and possibly the seediest 'zoo' in the world. Bukittinggi's pace of life is refreshingly sedate.

Embun Pagi offers the most spectacular view of Lake Maninjau, formed in a crater and one of the largest in the world. At first little can be seen — the thick clouds conceal the beauty below — but suddenly they make way for the splendour of Maninjau. The route downwards twists and turns with its forty–four bends until finally the lake appears. They say we have dropped over six hundred metres. Time for a dip, I think.

Monday, 11th February:
There are places in Asia — like Pagan and Luang Prabang — that make you sit back, relax and forget the world outside. Bukittinggi is just such a place.

Tuesday, 12th February:
How different from the 'Land of Smiles': for twelve thousand rupiah (just over three pounds) you get a great tour where no one's trying to flog you rubies, a massage or even their daughter.

South of Bukittinggi lies another lake, Singkarak which is smaller than Maninjau and can't quite boast the splendour of its sister. But we mustn't dwell by the lakeside sipping tea, there's much to be seen. There's the palace of the former King of the Minangkabau at Pagaruyung — a vast building with a truly splendid wooden pointed roof. And there's the town of Batusangkar, deemed the centre of the Minangkabau culture. And then there's the shopping . . . some of the most fantastic cloth you could ever hope to see. And they even take 'Visa'. What *do* the women make of that?

Bull against bull in a squelching quagmire of mud: the West Sumatrans idea of a fun afternoon. No bookmakers in sight but judging by the yelling and screaming a good few rupiah were changing hands. No one could tell me how to pick the winner: maybe it was size, or agility or just plain ferocity. The loser? Well he was the one who gave up first and fled the scene (a Siamese bull, possibly?) followed by one very angry ox and several irate punters. In their excitement and eagerness to get a better view, a number of spectators (mainly tourists) slipped on the mud and fell headlong into the ring. Each tumble was greeted with whoops of delight from the locals. Occasionally they would land within a few yards of the raging bulls: then, they would pick themselves up and run in terror out of the animals' eyeshot. Behind me, caged in a flimsy wooden stall, was the next contender. Every now and then, ominous snorts would emanate from within. The louder they got, the further I withdrew, until I was far enough away to avoid being gored.

The Three Tables Coffee House is actually a little more than that, but most of the menu is 'off'. The waiter, who scarcely speaks a word of English, is a strange looking character — an albino Indonesian. Everything in the kitchen is *"finis"*, he explains, everything, that is, except the spaghetti. I order a bowl of cold spaghetti with three dead ants in it and get a massage from a passing drunk. Such is Sumatra.

Thursday, 14th February:
Reluctantly we head back to Padang. From there we can get a direct flight to Singapore on Sunday. It's time for a bit of luxury and for Iew, hopefully, some 'tom yam'.

At the Mariani International Hotel, the staff (and handful of guests) are crowded round the television. They say the US bombed four hundred civilians in Iraq. Maybe it's not such a good time to be in South–East Asia, and particularly Muslim Indonesia. Yet I haven't detected any hostility or any difference between, say, the Buddhists of Laos or Burma and the Muslims of Sumatra. Indeed, wherever I've travelled, I have been greeted with nothing but extreme warmth and friendliness.

Friday, 15th February:
The route south of Padang leads to Bungus Bay: it twists and turns past waterfalls and rice–fields, and every now and then you can glimpse the sea. The Bay is deserted save for an old man who tries to sell me a trip in his boat to some distant island. I decline, preferring instead to sample the lukewarm waters of what I presume to be the Indian Ocean. No ladies, no boys, no 'kateuys', no massage. No worries.

Saturday, 16th February:
Padang's community, like that of so many South–East Asian towns, gravitates towards the market. Extraordinary numbers of cloth–stalls (the region specialises in a particularly beautiful type of hand–made material), clothes shops and fruit–stalls form the bulk of the market, but if you look hard

enough, you can lay you hands on almost any item. In my search for some cloth, I notice three Muslim women persistently following me about. They are from Malaysia and are keen to improve their English. So we take lunch together and talk: they are so timid and coy, but speak excellent English. They tell me they are studying in Padang but hope to come to England one day. We part and, as with so many of the people I have met since I started my travels, I am sure I will never see them again. Such is the all too brief joy and ensuing sadness of this existence.

Sunday, 17th February:
The confusion that could only be Tabing Airport, Padang: for Singapore, no schedule, no check–in counter, no idea. The information desk reveals that there should have been a flight at five minutes to ten this morning, but there wasn't. Or, there might have been, but the girl wasn't sure. The flight number doesn't correspond to that shown on my ticket and no one seems to care. Against my wishes, a scruffy looking individual wrestles my bags from me and disappears into a room at the back. Five minutes later, he re–emerges, demands my ticket and one thousand rupiah. I glean no more from him. Passport control merely offers a groan and a stamp; waiting beyond, however, in the departure lounge is a large group of Muslim women. They all have their faces covered, to avoid the sight, I sense, of the antique F–28 of Garuda Airlines which is snorting impatiently on the tarmac. What was the motto? 'Fly Garuda, die Garuda'.

Iew and I occupy the seats at the very rear of the aircraft, assuredly the two noisiest in aviation history. Garuda also has perfected the technique of encountering as much turbulence as is humanly possible. By the time we reach Changi Airport, my ears felt like they have just walked out of a rock concert.

Ah Singapore, home of Raffles, and South–East Asian civilisation. Where there's no graffiti, no crime, no vandalism. Singapore, where fines lurk round the corner for jaywalkers and those who spit in the streets. Where those who forget to flush a public toilet are fined one hundred and fifty Singapore dollars (three Singapore dollars equals one pound approximately) and litterbugs one thousand dollars (for a first offence). Smokers in prohibited areas — such as air–conditioned restaurants — escape with a mere five hundred dollar penalty, as do drivers who are caught leaving the country with less than three–quarters of a tank of petrol (this is to deter motorists from filling up in neighbouring Malaysia, where fuel is much cheaper). Vandals may be lashed: robbers, rapists and attempted murderers most certainly will be. 'Successful' murderers, kidnappers, drug traffickers and those caught with a gun, face death on the gallows. And all this in the land of the 'Singapore Sling'.

Heard about the new subway which was opened? It came equipped with a list of prohibitions. Smoking and playing radios or musical instruments were banned. So were eating or drinking, bringing animals, carrying 'large' luggage (now how *do* the authorities differentiate between 'large' and 'small' luggage?), hawking, and resting your feet on the plastic seats. All these 'offences' received a five hundred dollar fine. And the list was later amended to add a ban on chewing gum or 'being seen about to chew gum'. What *would* Raffles have made of it all?

Monday, 18th February:
I should have purchased my hotel voucher at Changi Airport. That way the hotel room would have been cheaper. Instead I'd followed the Thai example — which is, only check room availability at the airport, don't book: the counter charges vast commission. And so I was left temporarily without accommodation — and with egg on my face, a face I'd just lost too, I presume.

There's something about Singapore that makes you want to buy, buy, buy. And eat . . . some of the Chinese and Indian restaurants are just different class to those elsewhere in South–East Asia. Singapore is Hong Kong without the brusqueness and with a hundred times more charm. It may be clinical but it's got style. And if it weren't for the heat and humidity, you could be almost anywhere in the Western World. Indeed the very moment you touch down at the extraordinary construction that is Changi Airport (or 'Airtropolis' as the image–makers like to call it), you're transported out of Asia. And into an immense department store; only one full of Orientals.

Tuesday, 19th February:
Chinese New Year is a tremendously joyful occasion: there are parades and fairs, dances and parties. The town buzzes with excitement and, unlike the Thai 'Songkran', you don't get a drenching each time you step outside. Even if you did, at least you'd be able to drink the water . . . for this *is* Singapore.

Thursday, 21st February:
Laden with gifts, I am returning to Bangkok. I have been impressed with what I have seen so far. There may not be the spontaneity and natural exuberance of some of the other lands of the region, but Singapore has a character all of its own. And one that in certain respects her neighbours could do well to follow.

The China Airlines Airbus bounces us about wantonly: strange, the flight path to Don Muang is invariably turbulent. But this was something else: the woman opposite looked at me pleadingly, hoping to gain some solace. From me? I forced myself to smile back Thai-style: I don't think she could tell that I was just as terrified.

I head to the Thai Airways counter to cancel Iew's return ticket from Penang–Bangkok, which I was obliged to buy to enable him to leave the country in the first place. As chance would have it, the same surly shrew is on hand to welcome me to Bangkok, 'City of Angels', capital of the 'Land of Smiles'.

"I would like to cancel this ticket and get a refund please," I politely request. She remembers me all right. Let the battle of attrition commence.

"Not possible, sir," is her opening gambit.

"Why?"

"You must go head office." That should fob me off.

"Why? The ticket was issued here." A counter–thrust.

"Please wait, sir." She takes as long as she can, one by one consulting her colleagues before smugly concluding *"refund take one hour."*

"No problem. I wait." And I did, for forty minutes. And thus we both saved face.

Sukhumvit Road, Soi 2 is throbbing with activity. Who said the Gulf War was affecting business? The Nana Hotel is vibrant: touts, 'bar–girls', 'bar–boys', and 'undecideds'. At times like this, you wonder if there could possibly be life away from this inscrutable city — and if the Nana Hotel was really named after Zola's lascivious heroine? If not, it's a helluva coincidence.

Friday, 22nd February:
I am back in Bangkok, one task still to complete — getting Iew a visa for the UK. He might like it, too: Thailand is very much the fashion at home these days.

Or rather 'was' in, before Bangkok became a maze of international terrorism. *"Don't travel to Thailand unless you absolutely have to"* warns the Foreign Office in the UK. And what about those of us who have to wait seventeen days before securing an interview at the British Embassy in Bangkok? Get out of town, I suppose, destination Phuket.

If the streets of Bangkok were a racecourse, there would be more Stewards Inquiries than discarded bottles of Bollinger. Having been almost put over the rails by a deranged taxi–driver, our 'Isaan' 'tuk–tuk' driver, frenzied and wreaking vengeance, forces the taxi out of the race and into the haven of an adjoining 'soi'. Simple 'sanuk', served with a smile. Oh Bangkok, oriental city, maelstrom of madness, mayhem and mania.

Saturday, 23rd February:
And a downright disgrace. one hundred and thirty–two baht for a five second call to the UK. Who's fooling whom?

The arrivals hall at Phuket Airport but no sign of Iew's bag: apologies from the Thai Airways staff. They had forgotten to unload the luggage from the plane.

Contrary to reports, the War hasn't done much damage to Patong's tourist trade. The beach may not be quite as bustling — though the hopeful myriad of salesmen still plies its trade remorselessly along the sand — but the hotels and bars continue to prosper. And who could ever envisage that changing?

Welcome to Patong Beach Hotel, the hotel which looks out onto a building site. There's hardly a 'rai' of Patong left which hasn't been exploited, and my room just happens to adjoin a rapidly tumescent construction.

Sunday, 24th February:
"Revolution, revolution," announces Iew quite calmly to me, as I sit on the balcony enjoying my 'Gleen Spot' (I've moved room now, away from the concrete–mixers).
    "What do you mean revolution?"
    "Bangkok. Government go away. Chatichai go away," comes the explanation.

"Go away where?" I was having a little trouble following his broken English. So I switched on the TV and there it was, or rather wasn't. A picture of the Thai flag and military music. And then some army–looking man rambling on and on and on. Interminably. Now I understood: I had been in a coup d'état — and survived. And I didn't even have to hide under the bed to duck the bullets. Didn't even hear a shot. Will they think I'm a hero at home?

Monday, 25th February:
Patong Beach under martial law and nothing's changed. Hawkers still hawk, touts still tout and whores still whore. And all under the supervision of the military? Well not exactly; more like the Patong mafia.

Soi Bangla is where it's at — half a mile of 'bar–beers', restaurants and the notorious Crocodile Disco, where the men look like women and the women . . . like nothing better than nicking your wallet. After Bangkok and Pattaya, Phuket is Thailand's great honey–pot where the lasses come from far and wide to make their fortune and to hook a 'farang'. Patong is just so sleazy you can't fail to 'sanuk'.

Now, sexuality is a curious thing in Thailand. No one cares: unless you're a member of the government or aristocracy. Transvestism is a particularly common phenomenon. I wonder if any psychologist has examined this aspect of Thai society and discovered why so many Thai men are effeminate. Perhaps there's a link somewhere with Buddhism, the most tolerant of religions, and the Buddha's attitude to sex. Sex was neither good nor bad, nor was a man's sexual organ. I wonder if my masseuse had one: for she was most definitely a man once. Now she claims to be every inch (?) a woman.

Tuesday, 26th February:
It's become all too fashionable these days to run down Phuket, where sun, sea and sand have given way to sex, sleaze and videotape. But that's not entirely fair: in Phuket you get what you want. If you lock yourself away within the confines of the Phuket Yacht Club on Nai Harn Beach, you'll get nothing Thai, only lobster thermidor and some exotic cocktails. If you plump for Patong Beach, the possibilities are endless. You can drink yourself senseless dancing away the night to the strains of Joan Jett belting out the old Creedence Clearwater Revival hit *'Have You Ever Seen The Rain?'* Or, you can forget the world outside and retire to a life of dope, coconuts and Sunset Bungalows at forty baht a night. From where, with a pair of binoculars, you may even glimpse the rich 'farangs' sipping their 'Mai Tais' on the verandah of the Phuket Yacht Club.

"Hello handsome man, hello velly handsome 'falang', ooh velly, velly handsome man," shrieks each girl in turn in her best 'bar English' as she attempts to lure you into her joint. Yes, a 'bar–girl' is instantly recognis-

able by her idiosyncratic use of broken English and a swear word beginning with 'f'. And even if she doesn't open her mouth, she betrays a certain surly look that can only mean one thing: whore.

The inscrutable Thais: how often I've heard that expression. Has any 'farang' ever discovered what makes a Thai tick? Is it possible to do more than merely scratch the surface? And if so, what lies beneath? Whimsical, capricious, impetuous, moody, petulant, irrational, scheming, devious, cunning. Crazy. Has any Western psychologist, I wonder, ever probed the deeper recesses of the Thai mind? If he had, he would have found — in many cases — a child. Yes a kid, no less, masquerading as an adult. With a love of comics and slapstick and a puerile obstinacy. No motivation, no ambition but plenty of superstition. Flippancy, a curious and unhealthy obsession with gore, flatterers (others would say bullshitters). But one thing's for sure, at all times the Thais remain utterly unpredictable; fascinating, incalculable and unfathomable.

Wednesday, 27th February:
It could only be a Thai who has the name 'Bank'. Still, it's less of a mouthful than 'National Westminster'.

A tropical storm hits Patong. I foolishly take cover in a bar nearby where a couple of ageing hostesses sit, surveying the passing 'farang' trade with no real optimism. Until now, that is. For at long last their luck appears to have turned. These two could never be accused of diffidence.

"Ooh, handsome man," the bashful one begins, *"I love you already. You buy one beer for me, na?"*
   The other won't be outdone: *"You love me, na? You take me short time?"* In one shake of a lobster's tail, I was away, through the cats and dogs, oblivious of the lightning, until I reached the sanctuary of Patong Beach Bungalows.

Saturday, 2nd March:
I could have been part of the coup d'état. For it was I, one week ago, who sat waiting in the domestic terminal for my flight to Phuket as General Chatichai was being dethroned on the runway. I saw it all, I dodged the gunfire, I . . . must have had too many Singhas.
   "Why you look me? You love me? You think me beautiful, na?": yes, it's fatal to stare at anyone in this land of narcissism. I walk on. Perhaps the heat's getting to me.

Sunday, 3rd March:
I relax on the beach next to an Austrian couple: the girl, baring her oversized breasts, clearly has no understanding of Thai mores. Revealing your tits is just not done, nor is welching on a deal when you've agreed on a

price. Having haggled with an umbrella salesman, the stupid Fräulein from Linz changed her mind and reneged on the final sum of two hundred baht. Now that's worse than showing your boobs: she's changed her mind she tells the distraught salesman, who's halved the price from four hundred baht (even though you can get them for around one hundred in Chiang Mai). He becomes frantic:

"You agree two hundred baht. I sell you for two hundred baht. Now you say no. Why? You must buy for two hundred, we agree two hundred." And so it goes on: he is insistent she must honour her debt, she, completely unaware of Thai customs, couldn't care less about defaulting. Indeed the more angry he gets, the more determined she is not to buy. He even drops the price to one hundred and fifty baht. I had never imagined that business for the umbrella salesmen could be so bad. And how ironic that he should be wearing a T-shirt bearing the logo of a man swinging nonchalantly in a hammock between two coconut palms muttering: *"Ho hum, another shitty day in Paradise".*

His rage is such that he is almost in tears. So I intervene: I give him two hundred baht and take the damned umbrella. I feel like a gullible 'farang' as I walk up the beach with my Chiang Mai umbrella (which was probably made in Phuket) under my arm. Still, it's a better buy than a 'ruby' at two hundred dollars.

Tuesday, 5th March:
Forget Bangkok or Pattaya, Patong Beach must rank as *the* Thai bordello. Where marriage proposals are two a baht and ages vary from eight to eighty.

Wednesday, 6th March:
One year on from the cockroaches and vomit of the Miami Hotel. Now it's the lobsters, giant prawns and 'goong' of Patong Seafood Restaurant. What a debt we 'farangs' owe to the military junta. Oh that there were more coups . . . by the way, you couldn't pass me another crab claw?

Saturday, 9th March:
More idle days spent lying on the beach, lazing by the pool. Sipping a 'Mai Tai' or maybe a 'Singapore Sling'. Reflecting on the journeys, the hopes and aspirations, the future. The awesome splendour of Pagan, the mystique of Mandalay, the magnificent isolation of Luang Prabang. The madness of Chiang Mai seems but a distant memory.

Sunday, 10th March:
"Patong make me happy, make me sad, make me laugh, make me cry." So says Iew as we prepare to leave. And for once I agree.

Monday, 11th March:
Sukhumvit Road, Bangkok. The ultimate nightmare for any postman, as Thailand's longest road stretches from Soi 1, near the railway line, all the way to the Cambodian border. What Soi would that be? Telling someone you live on Sukhumvit Road is as imprecise and inexact as a Thai politician's bank statement.

The Nana Hotel, located at the beginning of Soi 4 and well placed for the British Embassy in nearby Thanon Wittayu, may not be as notorious as the Grace Hotel (in Soi 3), but it doesn't do at all badly. The Nana has tried to go upmarket, but since it lies right opposite the sleazy Nana Complex, self–aggrandisement isn't really possible. Nonetheless it's a good deal less murky than the Grace and its infamous coffee shop, an Arab oasis in the Orient. Exotic, bizarre, weird.

Sukhumvit is rapidly becoming *the* tourist area of Bangkok, with 'farangs', at times, almost outnumbering the Thais. There's everything from the vast Ambassador complex (one thousand and fifty rooms, fourteen restaurants and disco) to 'short–time' hotels at fifty baht a bonk; eating–houses from the fabulous Lemongrass to the oddly named Cabbages and Condoms . . . and Soi Cowboy, the Patpong of Sukhumvit.

It's a relief stepping into a 'tuk–tuk' on Soi 4 and simply requesting *"Bai satahn toot angrit tao lai kup?"* (*"How much to the British Embassy?"*) — I can form whole sentences now, without the assistance of a Maekhong — for it's a mere thirty baht away, just ten minutes even in the rush hour.

The Embassy is guarded by two sullen individuals, heavily armed and twice the width of the average Thai. There are persistent rumours of a terrorist attack in the city and warnings abroad not to travel to the Kingdom. The British Embassy is an obvious target which, coupled with the fear of terrorism and the coup, would be one more nail in Thailand's tourist coffin. Inside it is a very different scene: a microcosm of a brothel. Hopeful 'bar–girls' with British boy–friends, or husbands for the lucky ones, 'bar–boys', and the odd 'kateuy' (whom Iew now refers to as 'kateuy pacific', having been both amused and confused by the sight of a Cathay Pacific jet on the runway of Seoul Airport). Most will be disappointed.

Waiting just outside the Embassy was a young girl from Udon. She was trying to get a visa to spend a holiday with her sister who was married to a 'farang'. She couldn't understand a word of English and didn't have a clue how to complete the form. She didn't really know why she wanted to go either, but she thought she'd try. It was fortunate that a 'farang' was on hand to fill out her application form: I got the impression she'd have been prepared to wait all day for help if necessary. I never found out whether she got a visa, but most of the girls there didn't.

They all had their dreams, their fantasies, their fabricated stories. And not one could understand why they'd been so heartlessly thwarted. I'd seen them pray to Buddha just before an interview, often in vain. Iew had a quick pray, too, just to be on the safe side, just in case. *"Buddha take care of you?"* I asked him. *"I think so."* And with that, he was summoned into the interview room.

After ten minutes or so, he reappeared. *"Now you go inside,"* he said. *"Buddha take care of me too?"* I inquired. *"Maybe."*

Behind the glass partition that separated Thai and tourist from official 'farang', was a young civil servant from Bath on his first posting abroad. *"Now Mr Greenwood, you wouldn't mind my asking you a few questions? Tell me about the book you're writing . . ."* Yes, sir; this is it.

Buddha had come up with the goods.

Tuesday, 12th March:
I don't think Iew fully appreciates what is happening to him. Nonetheless, he hastily packs a small bag, bids goodbye to me and hops into a 'tuk–tuk', destination: the Northern Bus Terminal. He's decided to return to 'Isaan' for a day to say 'sawatdee' to his family. A whirlwind visit, conceived in an inkling. Oh so Siamese. He comes back tomorrow by plane. Such is the life of a nouveau riche Thai.

Wednesday, 13th March:
Iew flies in from Sakhon Nakhon: on his wrists are tied several pieces of white thread. This is known as 'sai sin' and is a custom especially prevalent

in 'Isaan'. It is deemed to bring you good luck and protect you from the spirits. 'Samlor' drivers in Bangkok (many of whom came originally from the North–East) are often seen sporting 'sai sin'. And they need to!

"Yesterday have big party for me in my how me. Everybody give money me and say goodbye. Everybody mao." He then cut off the threads and threw them into the rubbish bin. I hope he hasn't angered the 'Phi': I was always told the 'sai sin' should be kept on for at least three days.

For one last time I disappear into the stench of the 'City of Angels' to buy Iew a ring as a leaving present (for Thais, the more expensive the better, but they must be of gold — then they can pawn them when they encounter bad times). I hesitate in front of the shop, which I cannot bring myself to enter. For, written in big letters is the name 'Anuphong Silver Jewery and gem's'. I flee the scene.

Though he's discarded his 'sai sin', Iew certainly can't complain about the 'Phi' so far. They've been good to him, and to me too, I suppose. But for now, though, our oriental journey has come to an end, the adventure is over. As for Iew, well with or without the spirits, his story could just be beginning.

We flew out of Don Muang Airport during the early hours of Thursday, 14th March 1991. On board the Boeing 767 of Scandinavian Airlines System were thirty Vietnamese refugees — mainly children — also starting a new life in the West.

POSTSCRIPT

Iew has been having 'sanuk' and improving his English at a language school in London. John Davies obtained a UK visa for Rin and for a (brief) while they lived quite peacefully just outside Salisbury. However, in true Chiang Mai style, things didn't work out as anticipated and their relationship has run its full course. Indeed, as irony would have it, Iew and I acted as witnesses to their 'divorce' at the Thai Embassy in London. Rin subsequently appears to have remarried. John's third book, *Touring Northern Thailand*, is complete. What further adventures, I wonder, lie ahead?

GLOSSARY

A

Akha   Known to the Thais as the 'Ekaw', the Akha originated in Yunnan province in South China and settled first in Thailand in 1903. They number around twenty-eight thousand, wear an essentially black costume with a stunning head-dress and tend to be situated in a relatively small area north of Chiang Rai.

Aloy   Tasty, in Thai. More properly pronounced 'aroy'.

Angrit   England or English, in Thai.

Arai?   Thai for 'what?' 'Arai na kup?' means the same but is more polite and is also colloquial, if that isn't a contradiction in terms.

Aung San Suu Kyi   See NLD.

B

Baht   The Thai unit of currency, divided into one hundred satang. It is fairly stable, and fluctuates little against the dollar – generally hovering around the twenty–five mark. It varies more against the pound – anything from between forty to fifty.

Bai nai?   Frequent Thai greeting, literally meaning 'where you go?' Thais often use 'bai nai?' rather than 'Hello' or 'How are you?'

Bai tio   A favourite Thai pastime, just strolling about seeing what's what, maybe shopping, eating or drinking – indeed anything that's just 'sanuk'.

Bangkok Post   Quality English newspaper printed daily in Bangkok. Its rival is called *The Nation*. Both cost ten baht.

Bar-beer   Should be the other way round: it's a Thai beer bar. A very basic construction offering booze, loud music and (often) prostitutes.

Bar-boy   A Thai lad who works in a bar (of any description) as a prostitute.

Bar-girl   Same as above, only female. The girls, often from the North-East, can be 'offed' (taken out) from the bar for a 'bar fee' and the rest, as they say, is 'up to you'. In many of the Bangkok bars, the girls have a number pinned on their swimsuit (or whatever they wear): some say it's to make it all official, others say it's to stop the customer having to point at the girl he's chosen (pointing of course, being supposedly taboo in Thailand).

Bin   The Thai pronounciation of 'bill': one of the ways of requesting the bill in Thailand is to say "check bin kup."

Bpaat   Eight. (Thai).

Butterfly   A man or woman who plays the field: that's to say someone who isn't faithful and sleeps around. Literally, a pretty thing that flits from flower to flower. Thais often say 'butterfry'.

C

Cam on nhieu   Vietnamese for 'thank you very much'.

Casey   Thai pronounciation of the English word 'crazy'.

Chatichai   Elected in 1988, Chatichai Choonhavan was the Prime Minister of Thailand until being overthrown in a military coup on February 23rd, 1991.

Chedi   Architectural feature of a Thai temple. A tall structure shaped rather like a hand-bell and usually painted white. Called in India a 'stupa', it generally houses a valuable relic or the ashes of an eminent (and devout) person.

Chezu tinbada   'Thank you' in Burmese.

Chohk dee   Thai for 'good luck'.

Cyclo   Also known as a rickshaw, trishaw or sidecar.

D

Dong   The Vietnamese currency, the highest denomination of which is the five thousand dong note. There are no coins. One US dollar is a little over six thousand dong.

Don Muang   Bangkok International Airport, about twenty-five kilometres north of the city.

Dtah   Eye. (Thai).

F

Farang   One of the most common words you'll hear on your travels in Thailand, meaning Caucasian or Westerner. It often has a pejorative ring to it, despite what some commentators might say.

Fido Dido   A cartoon-type character used to advertise 'Sprite' or 'Seven Up'. His motif is often seen on T-shirts.

Flee   Thai pronounciation of 'free'.

Flee the scene   Drivers involved in accidents will often run away from the scene to avoid being caught and thus losing face.

Fontok mak mak kao kang nai dee kwar   It's raining heavily, you better come in. (Thai).

G

Gairo   Drinking glass. (Thai).

Gai yang   Barbecued chicken. A favourite of North-East Thailand.

Gao   Nine. (Thai).

Geh how   Thai pronounciation of 'guest house'.

Gin kao   Literally Thai for 'eat rice', used simply to mean 'eat'.

Gleen Spot   The Thai pronounciation for 'Green Spot', their version of the fizzy orange drink 'Fanta'.

Goong   The Thai generic term for prawns or shrimps.

H

Hah   Five. (Thai).

Hahng   Tail. (Thai).

Hang Khong Viet Nam   Nobody in their right mind flies on Vietnam's national airline: here, for example is a recent notice taken from the magazine *Air International*. Jan 12 1991: Vietnam Airlines TU-134A VN-A126: 'Made heavy landing at Ho Chi Minh City after flight from Bangkok and severely damaged left main gear. No injuries reported but damage to aircraft subsequently found to be more extensive and declared a write-off'.

Hmong   Known as Meo to the Thais, the Hmong originate from South China and are the second largest hilltribe. In Thailand they are essentially divided into White and Blue Hmong, which refer to the colours of their costumes. They number around seventy thousand in Thailand and there are over two hundred and fifty villages.

Hohk   Six. (Thai).

I J

Isaan   North-East Thailand.

Jai dee   Literally 'good heart': kind, generous. (Thai).

Jet   Seven. (Thai).

K

Kamoy   Thief. (Thai).

Kao   Rice, the staple diet of the Thais. Generally either 'kao suay', steamed rice, or 'kao niaow', glutinous or 'sticky' rice. The latter is normally eaten in Northern and North-East Thailand.

Karen   The largest hilltribe in Thailand with a population of about three hundred thousand – and almost five million in Burma. They are divided into two groups Skaw and Pwo, each with a different language.

Kateuy   Also called 'ladyboy': a transvestite or an effeminate man. (Thai).

Kaw tohd   'Excuse me' or 'I'm sorry'. (Thai).

Kee niaow   Literally 'sticky shit', by extension, miserly or mean. (Thai).

Khantoke   A 'traditional' Northern Thai meal accompanied by dancing – i.e. a tourist rip-off, best avoided.

Khon dtor bai kup   'Next please' (Thai).

Khun kroo   How Thais refer to a teacher.

Kip   The Laotian currency.

Kop jai   'Thank you' in Lao.

Kop koon kup   'Thank you' in Thai, for a male speaker. Females say 'kop koon ka'.

Krung Thep   Thais call Bangkok 'Krung Thep', the 'City of Angels'. Only when talking to a non-Thai will they refer to the capital as Bangkok.

Kuomintang   Chinese refugees from the communist revolution of 1949. They make up the bulk of the population of Doi Mae Salong, a small town in Northern Thailand.

Kup Often written in English as 'khrap', it is the polite form in Thai, spoken by a male, and coming at the end of the sentence. Females (and 'kateuys') use the word 'ka' instead. In certain contexts it also means 'yes'. Thus 'khrap, khrap, khrap' can be translated as 'yes, yes, yes' and not as 'no bloody good'.

Kyat The Burmese currency, pronounced 'chat'.

L

Lahu The Lahu had their origins in South-Western China and moved to Thailand from North East Burma after about 1880. They number around fifty–five thousand and have settled along the Burmese border, north of Chiang Mai. Most Lahu belong to the Black or Red linguistic group.

Lanna The Lanna Kingdom was established by King Mengrai on his accession to the throne of Chiang Saen in 1259. Chiang Mai was later to become its capital. Lanna literally means 'land of a million rice fields'.

Lao Thais call Laos or Laotian 'Lao'.

Lao Aviation Lao Aviation, the national airline of Laos, changed its name to Lao International in July 1991. At the same time the company introduced its first Tupolev TU-154M (now *there's* progress) into service between Vientiane and Bangkok. Other route plans include new services to Ho Chi Minh City and Kunming. Maybe the Tupolev replaced the AN-24, which, on April 22nd 1991, 'failed to become airborne due to overloaded condition, overran runway and crashed into building, killing one person on the ground.' Excess 'sticky' rice, perhaps?

Lao lao Laotian rice whisky: fearsome.

Larb Traditional 'Isaan' salad made of ground beef, (or chicken, pork, duck, fish) with chillies, mint and coriander leaves, fish sauce, lime juice, spring onions and cucumber.

Largon The Thai equivalent of 'adieu' in French. 'Farewell' rather than 'good-bye'.

Lek Little, small. (Thai).

Lisu In many ways the most interesting of all the hilltribes. The women wear the most colourful costumes and they can often be spotted selling their handicrafts at the Night Bazaar in Chiang Mai. The Lisu, who had their origins in Eastern Tibet and first arrived in Thailand in 1921, are the main opium cultivators in the Kingdom. They number around twenty–four thousand and their villages are situated near the Burmese border north of Chiang Mai and west of Chiang Rai.

Longyi A type of sarong worn by Burmese men and women.

M

Macharm Tamarind. (Thai).

Maekhong Thai whisky, molasses-based.

Mai aloy Not tasty. (Thai).

Mai ao 'I don't want': the best response to any hawker who is pestering you on Patong Beach.

Mai ben lai Normally written 'Mai pen rai'. Perhaps the most common phrase in the Thai language. Ostensibly it means 'never mind', 'don't worry', 'no problem' or 'you're welcome' (in response to 'thank you very much'). But in reality the meaning goes much deeper than that. 'Mai ben lai' is part of the Thai mentality, the laid-back, relaxed, procrastinatory way of Buddhism. It is a state of mind, what will happen will happen, conflict-avoidance; quite simply 'it doesn't matter'. 'Jai yen' – a cool heart – as opposed to 'jai lorn', a hot heart.

Mai dai Can't, cannot. (Thai).

Mai dee Not good, bad. (Thai).

Mai glai 'Not far' in Thai – as opposed to 'mai glai' which means 'not near'! Funny language. So don't ask a drunk if something is 'near' or 'far' as in Thai they are the same word only with a different tone.

Mai lu Don't know. (Thai).

Mai suay Not beautiful. (Thai).

Mao Drunk, intoxicated. (Thai).

Mingala baa 'Hello' in Burmese.

Moi ming hai 'Hello' in Yao.

Moo Pig or pork in Thai.

Motoby Thai pronounciation of the English word 'motorbike'.

Muay Thai Thai boxing: particularly vicious form of boxing, where (almost) anything goes. Sometimes called 'kick boxing'.

N

Na A word the Thais tag on to a sentence. Difficult to translate, it is roughly the equivalent of 'isn't it?' or 'eh?' in the sense "good, isn't it?" or "bad, eh?" Thais will say "arai na kup?" – "What is/was that?", "aloy na kup?" – "tasty?" and, another example, "chohk dee na kup", which simply means "good luck".

Nam pla Thai fish sauce, used in many everyday dishes.

Nam prik ong A Northern Thai speciality: a spicy dish of minced pork.

NLD National League for Democracy. In May 1990, this Burmese political party, under the leadership of Aung San Suu Kyi, won over eighty per cent (392 out of 485 seats) of the vote at the general election. However, the ruling military refused to hand over power and Aung San Suu Kyi remained under house arrest. In October 1991, Aung San Suu Kyi was awarded the Nobel Peace Prize.

Ne Win Also known euphemistically as 'Number One', 'The Old Man' or just 'He', Burmese general who led a successful coup d'état in 1962 against the democratic government of U Nu. An evil, xenophobic, neurotic, superstitious megalomaniac who has bankrupted the country (for example spending the nation's wealth on Soko G-4 Super Galeb advanced jet trainers, Chengdu F-7M fighters and Shenyang F-6 Squadrons) and, though officially retired, is still believed to pull the military strings. Most Burmese are eagerly awaiting his death in the hope that democracy will rise up from his ashes.

There are numerous tales about Ne Win, bandied about behind closed doors. Most illustrate the absurdity of his rule and, naturally, ridicule him. There is the story of a visit Ne Win paid one day to his presidential farm to inspect the produce, most notably his mango trees. The employees, fearful of Ne Win's wrath were he to discover that his tree was bereft of mangoes (most had already fallen to the ground) climbed up the tree with balls of string and proceeded to tie the mangoes back onto the branches. Ne Win could thus inspect his mango tree with pride and affection.

This tale may well be apocryphal, but it sums up the fear Ne Win has instilled into his countrymen, and how they attempted to appease him and keep him happy – even if, at all times, he was misinformed, misguided and hopelessly out of touch.

Nit noy   Thai for 'a little'.
Nung   One, in Thai.

P

Pah-see   Tax. (Thai).
Passart   Mad. (Thai).
Patpong   Notorious red-light area in Bangkok.
Pet mak mak   Very hot or spicy in Thai.
Phi   A Thai spirit – not the type you drink (see next entry).
Phi Tong Luang   The Spirits of the Yellow Leaves, also known as 'Yumbri' or 'Mlabri'. A small tribe, numbering around a hundred, only to be found in a few remote areas of Nan province in Northern Thailand. They are so-called because they construct their shelters out of leaves and when the leaves turn yellow they move on.

R

Rai   Thai unit of land measure, a square area equal to sixteen hundred square metres. One 'rai' equals 0.396 acres, one acre 2.53 'rai'.
Riel   Cambodian unit of currency.
Rupiah   Indonesian unit of currency.

S

Sabai dee   'Hello' in Laotian.
Sahm   Three, in Thai.
Sairp lai   Very tasty in Laotian; the Thais say 'aroy' ('aloy').
Sai sin   White threads tied around the wrists to bring good luck. A common 'Isaan' custom.
Sanuk   Literally 'enjoyment', but, as with 'mai ben lai', 'sanuk' has a deeper meaning than mere 'enjoyment'. According to the Thais, everything in life must be 'fun', 'sanuk'. If not, then it's 'mai sanuk' and, more often

than not, they won't do it. I found this out in Rin's when a new waitress left after less than a day's work because, quite simply, it was not 'sanuk'.

Satahn toot   Embassy, in Thai.

Sawatdee   'Hello' or 'good-bye' in Thai.

Shan   The second biggest ethnic group in Burma having the same origins as the Thais (from Yunnan province). They live in the mountain ranges between Burma and Thailand.

'Short time'   If you've ever been to Thailand and seen hotel rooms with curtains outside, you may have wondered what they were. Were they there to keep the cars clean? No, the curtains are pulled when a car drives in to conceal the identity of the occupant. For he – or she – is about to embark on a 'quickie' or go 'short time'. Not all 'short time' hotels have drive-ins with curtains, some just look like ordinary – if invariably run-down – hotels. So they tell me . . .

Si   Four. (Thai).

Singha   Thai beer.

Sip   Ten. (Thai).

SLORC   State Law and Order Restoration Council – the non-elected ruling military in Burma.

Sockapock   Dirty in Thai.

Soi   Lane: in Thailand a main road is called 'thanon' and has several lanes, or 'sois', running off it. The odd and even numbered 'sois' are on opposite sides of the 'thanon'.

Somtam   Often called 'papaya pok-pok' by the Thais ('pok-pok' being the sound of the pestle pounding the chillies in the mortar), this is a North-Eastern speciality of unripe papaya, chillies, dried prawns and peanuts – and lashings of 'nam pla', fish sauce. A proper 'Isaan' 'somtam' is 'pet mak mak': bloody hot.

Song   Two, in Thai.

Songkran   The Thai New Year, which takes place between April 13th and 15th (and in remote places often before and after these dates) and best witnessed in Chiang Mai. 'Songkran' is the Water Festival when Thais sprinkle water on Buddha images (as an act of purification) – and on everything else, particularly 'farangs'. Not to be confused with the Thai word for war – 'songkrahm', though at times there is little difference between the two.

Songthaew   A Thai open-sided pick-up truck with a row of seats down each side. They generally operate along set routes within towns as well as going to towns and villages in outlying areas. Fares are fixed, according to the distance you're travelling. 'Songthaew' literally means 'two rows', referring to the two benches in the rear.

T

Tack   Thai pronounciation of the word 'tax': Thais often fail to enunciate the final part of an English word – e.g. 'geh how' for 'guest house'.

Tao lai   Thai for 'how much?', correctly pronounced 'tao rai'.

Tatmadaw   The Burmese military who, if the red sign in Mandalay is to be believed, will 'never betray the National cause'.

Terima kasih   'Thank you' in Bahasa Indonesia.

TG   Airline symbol for Thai Airways International. (Others are QV: Lao Aviation, UB: Burma Air, etc).

Thanon   Road or street in Thai.

Theravada   The original (pure) school of Buddhism.

Tom yam   Spicy Thai soup flavoured with lemon grass, chillies, kaffir lime leaves, coriander, fish sauce ('nam pla'), lime juice and straw mushrooms. The most popular version is 'tom yam goong' – 'goong' being prawns – but it can be made with any seafood or chicken.

Tuk-tuk   Also known in Thailand as 'samlor' (literally 'three wheels'), the tuk-tuk is an alternative to a taxi or 'songthaew'. So-called because of the noise of its frequently applied horn. Driven by maniacs, often from 'Isaan'.

W Y

Wai   The traditional Thai form of greeting: two hands held together as in prayer and a slight bow of the head. The higher the hands are held, and the lower the head is bowed, the more respectful the 'wai'.

Wittayu   Wireless. (Thai).

Won   The South Korean currency.

Yao   Also known as the Mien, the Yao hilltribe had their origins in Southern China over two hundred years ago. Most Yao live east of Chiang Mai in Nan, Phayao and Chiang Rai provinces. There are about forty thousand living in Thailand.

SUGGESTED READING

Abbott, Gerry:
Back to Mandalay, Impact Books, 1990.

Beery, Galen:
Basic Spoken Lao in Sixteen Lessons, Charles E. Tuttle Company, 1977.

Boyes, Jon:
A Life Apart, Suriwong Books, 1989.
Hmong Voices, Suriwong Books, 1990.

Bradley, David:
Burmese Phrasebook, Lonely Planet Publications, 1988.

Cohen, Barbara:
The Vietnam Guidebook, Harper & Row, 1990.

Cooper, Robert and Nanthapa:
Culture Shock, Thailand, Times Books International, 1986.

Davies, John R:
A Trekkers Guide to: the Hill Tribes of Northern Thailand, Footloose Books, 1990.
Thailand: a Hilltribe Phrase Book, Footloose Books, 1990.

Dawood, Dr Richard:
Travellers' Health: How To Stay Healthy Abroad,
Oxford University Press, 1990

Kahrs, Kurt:
Thai Cooking, The Apple Press, 1990.

Lintner, Bertil:
Outrage, White Lotus, 1990.

Morris, Sallie:
South-East Asian Cookery, Grafton Books, 1989.

O'Brien, Harriet:
Forgotten Land, Michael Joseph, 1991.

Robertson, Richard:
Robertson's Practical English-Thai Dictionary,
Charles E Tuttle Company, 1987.

Robinson, Daniel:
Vietnam, Laos & Cambodia - a travel survival kit,
Lonely Planet Publications, 1991.

Wheeler, Tony:
Burma, a travel survival kit, Lonely Planet Publications, 1988.

Zickgraf, Ralph:
Laos, Chelsea House Publishers, 1991.

APPENDIX

Below is a country-by-country list of a few hotels, restaurants, bars and travel agents which, during the course of my travels, offered service and friendliness beyond the normal call of duty. I apologise if some of the addresses aren't precise – but that's South-East Asia for you.

BURMA

'Royal Orchid Tea' Shop, Mandalay. (If you want to meet Burmese students).

INDONESIA (SUMATRA)

BUKITTINGGI   Benteng Hotel No 1, Benteng St. Tel: (0752) 21115, situated near the Fort de Kock. (Couldn't be friendlier or more helpful. They also organise tours).
PADANG   Mariani International Hotel JL. Bundo Kandung 35. Tel: (0752) 25410.

LAOS

VIENTIANE   Le Souriya Restaurant (Thanon Pang Kham) and **Nam Phou Restaurant** (Fountain Circle off the same Thanon) – two excellent French eating-houses.

MALAYSIA

PENANG   Cathay Hotel 15 Leith Street, Georgetown. Tel: (04) 626271.

SINGAPORE

Annalakshmi Excelsior Hotel & Shopping Centre, 02-10, 5 Coleman Street, Singapore 0617. (Superb vegetarian Indian cuisine and outstanding service).
Tourist World Travel Service Pte Ltd 190 Clemenceau Avenue, 03-30 Singapore Shopping Centre, Singapore 0923. Tel: 3382357. Ask for Carol Foo. (Helpful and highly efficient).

THAILAND

BANGKOK
Red Corner Restaurant Sukhumvit Soi 7. (An extensive range of Thai and Western dishes).
Siam Wings Co Ltd 173/1-3 Suriwong Road, Bangrak, Bangkok 10500. Tel: 235-4757/8. Ask for Nisa Chalakkang. (Efficient travel company, a short 'tuk-tuk' ride from Patpong. Also has a resident lawyer).

Telephone Restaurant 114/11–13 Silom Soi 4 (often known as 'Patpong 3' or 'Soi Kateuy'). Tel: 2343279. Excellent Thai food, friendly atmosphere, smart staff. Almost opposite the Rome Club disco.

CHIANG MAI
Darngwean Restaurant Superhighway. (This is the extraordinary Thai restaurant: the name has never been written in English script so this is an approximate transliteration. Its actual location is one kilometre east of the airport junction on the Superhighway. Happy hunting).
Jade Lotus Chinese Restaurant 41 Moon Muang Road. Tel: (053) 212309. (Outstanding Chinese food and service).

PHUKET
Kwantong Seafood Restaurant off Beach Road, Patong. (To find this small but very friendly place, take the first left turn after the Phuket Cabana, that's in the direction away from the hubbub of Patong, and it's a few yards down on the right. A must).
Lai Mai Restaurant 86/15 Thawiwong Road, Patong. (First-rate food and great ice-cream).
P&P Bar (Unpretentious bar run by a Thai who speaks fluent German and excellent English. Head towards Kwantong, but turn right at the junction, and it's located on the right, a minute or so by foot).

VIETNAM
Ho Chi Minh If it's possible, ask for the guide Nguyen Ngoc Sang, Saigontourist, 49 Le Thanh Ton Street, Tel 98914. (Highly knowledgeable, well read, cultured and charming).